The
FRIENDSHIP
BOOK

of Francis Gay

D. C. THOMSON & CO., LTD.
London   Glasgow   Manchester   Dundee

A Thought
For Each Day
In 1975

If there be beauty in a world of ill,
  A quiet valley where a church bell rings,
Where there is faith and love and little homes,
  Speak on these things.
                                        Edna Jaques

REWARD

Our manes are plaited and our trappings gleam,
With well-groomed coats we make a splendid team.
And for our patience we deserve a treat,
A handful of sweet-smelling hay to eat.

DAVID HOPE

A

TIME TO CHAT

The village street, when neighbours meet,
Is just the place to spread the news —
Next Friday's dance, some new romance,
Or where to buy the children's shoes.
There's always time to have a chat
About important things like that.

DAVID HOPE

JANUARY

EDNA JAQUES, of Willowdale, Ontario, is
a poet whose verses have given comfort and
cheer to a host of Canadians and Americans.

This is a verse from her " Prayer for the New
Year."

Tonight I pray that this New Year shall bring
No sudden riches . . . only just enough
For every day's small need — a warm, clean bed,
Strength for the going, be it smooth or rough,
And always, God, a light to guide and bless,
And in my heart a song . . . for happiness.

A FRIEND told me this story of Jill Allen, a
blind girl from Southend.

Jill is used to people offering to guide her over
busy roads. So it came as no surprise to her when
she heard a voice beside her say, " Can I take
your arm ?"

With a smile, Jill agreed, thankful that someone
had thought of helping her. But as they crossed
the road, she realised the person holding her arm,
an elderly woman, walked slowly and with difficulty.
When they reached the pavement safely, Jill turned
to thank the stranger, but instead, the stranger
thanked Jill. " I'm so grateful to you for helping
me over the road," the old body said. " You see,
I've been ill, and this is the first time I've been
out !" And off she went.

I'm sure you can understand why, to Jill, that
passing incident in a busy street left a glow in
her heart.

FRIDAY—JANUARY 3.

ONE of the most useful inventions is the cat's eyes built into the road. But you can see them shine only at night, lit up by the reflection from the car lights.

The stars are always shining, but you see them only when darkness falls.

We take so many things for granted and it is only when we pass through a dark time we learn to appreciate them. A friend in need is a friend indeed, we say. Water is precious to the thirsty, food to the hungry, health to the stricken, comfort to the lonely, faith in the day of trial.

They are always there, but sometimes we only come to see them when we pass through the dark.

SATURDAY—JANUARY 4.

BETTY was five.

She was thrilled—not simply because of the presents and cards, but because it meant she'd be taking round the collection bowl at her Sunday school in Lothian Road Church, Edinburgh, for the honour goes to the child with a birthday during the week.

Well, Betty duly took the offering. Afterwards, she ran all the way home to tell her mother about it. But as Mum hung up Betty's coat, a 2p piece fell from her pocket.

" Betty," exclaimed her mother, " you forgot to put in your own collection !"

" I didn't forget," retorted Betty. " There was plenty of money in the bowl without mine !"

SUNDAY—JANUARY 5.

WITH God nothing shall be impossible.

THE FRIENDSHIP BOOK

MONDAY—JANUARY 6.

DID you know that no woman can be married to the same man for fifty years? After the first twenty-five, he's a different man!

So I've been told, anyway. Do you agree?

TUESDAY—JANUARY 7.

MRS MARGARET McILWRAITH, of Kilmarnock, sat at the bedside of her little girl, Margaret, only three years old, but critically ill and not expected to live.

On holiday a few months before, Margaret was scampering happily about the beach. Then, early in October, her parents were told she had only a little while left.

Only those who have ever lost a child can fully understand how Mrs McIlwraith felt. Then her oldest boy came to her with his treasured autograph book, open at the front page, and there his grandpa had written:

It is not given to man to know
Just how life's winding path will go;
He cannot guess, but happy he
Whose faith goes forth triumphantly.

It was like a voice from beyond, assuring her that dark though the way might be, the shining lantern of faith could carry her through it.

WEDNESDAY—JANUARY 8.

*F*ORGET *the things that, through the year,*
Contrived to make you sad;
Remember only happy days,
On which your heart was glad.
Fresh courage take — cast out your fear,
And bravely meet another year.

THURSDAY—JANUARY 9.

HOW much sad news should children read in newspapers? How much should we hide from them? A young married friend of ours was worried when her children read the sad tale of how a woman, driven to despair by threats of war and unrest, walked into the sea with her young children.

She thought her own youngsters shouldn't be introduced to the sorrows of the world so early, and hoped they would soon put the item out of their minds. Imagine her surprise when one day, months later, one of them said to her, " Mummy, remember that poor lady who drowned herself? Well, if she'd just waited, everything would have been all right."

Sometimes children see things more clearly.

FRIDAY—JANUARY 10.

A TRAVELLING missionary was visiting a new church in Africa, and, as he was being shown round, he remarked on the absence of any form of lighting. The pastor of the church smiled and said that they didn't need any. The visitor was mystified until it came to the time for evening worship and the pastor led him to the door of the church and pointed to a long line of twinkling lights making their way towards the church. As each worshipper entered the building, he put his little lamp down at the end of the row, until everybody was in and the whole church bright with hundreds of small lights.

The missionary was reminded of two lines in that simple hymn " Jesus bids us shine."

In this world is darkness; so let us shine,
You in your small corner, and I in mine.

THE FRIENDSHIP BOOK

*NOW here's to you and yours, to wish
    You health, good luck, good cheer.
May they be yours abundantly,
    Throughout the dawning year.
And if the way be hard, may you
Have grace and strength to battle through.*

REJOICE with them that do rejoice, and weep with them that weep.

ONE Sunday the minister ended his sermon with these words : " Practical religion means praying on your knees and being useful on your feet."

In the spring of 1941 I was spending a Sunday in a small Scottish Lowland town. I went to church in the evening, and enjoyed the short and simple service attended by less than a score of folk.

Darkness had not quite fallen when we came out, and the congregation split up into small groups, chatting for a moment or two. Francis Gay was standing very much alone.

Then a country woman, bless her, detached herself from a group and came over to me. She said, " You'll be a stranger around here, likely ? "

I said I was, and that I had arrived on Saturday evening and would be off in the morning.

She nodded. " Well," said she, " if you'd care to come home wi' me, there'll be a cup of tea ; and my man, who's an invalid, will enjoy having somebody to talk to."

Said I to myself that memorable evening : " This is practical religion ! "

TUESDAY—JANUARY 14.

LET me tell you about Princess Eugenie of Sweden. She sold all her jewels to provide a Home for Incurables. On one of her visits to the Home she met one of the older women to whom she talked about Jesus. She told the matron, on leaving, that she hoped special attention would be paid to that poor creature, for the Princess was anxious that before the woman died, she would become a Christian.

One day some time later the Princess found the old woman wreathed in smiles. She was radiant with her new hope. She had given herself at last to Jesus. That evening the Princess, with tears in her eyes when she returned to the palace, said to her husband, " Today I saw the glitter of my diamonds."

WEDNESDAY—JANUARY 15.

GRANDPARENTS can often be a pest when you're trying to bring up a family.

Even those who were strict with their own children tend to spoil their grandchildren terribly.

Of course, they do provide a good baby-sitting service and fill in all the gaps that busy mums and dads can't fill.

But just how do you strike a happy balance ?

One little four-year-old girl I know, continually told her parents she was going to live with her grandparents because, " They are nicer than you are."

At breakfast one time she said to her father, " I was going to go last night after you smacked me and put me to bed."

" Why didn't you, then ?" he asked, exasperated.

She shrugged. " I didn't know what number bus to get."

THURSDAY—JANUARY 16.

I CAME across these lines the other day. They were published in the Bulletin of Balham Rectory a few years ago, but I think you'll agree they still apply :

Ten little churchmen went to church when fine;
But it started raining, then there were nine.
Nine little churchmen stayed up very late;
One overslept himself, then there were eight.
Eight little churchmen on the road to Heaven;
One joined a cycling club, then there were seven.
Seven little churchmen heard of Sunday flicks;
One thought he'd like to go, then there were six.
Six little churchmen kept the place alive;
One bought television, then there were five.
Five little churchmen seemed loyal to the core;
The minister upset one, then there were four.
Four little churchmen asked out to tea;
One couldn't leave in time, then there were three.
Three little churchmen sang the service through;
Got a hymn they didn't know, then there were two.
Two little churchmen argued who should run
The annual bazaar, then there was one.

FRIDAY—JANUARY 17.

MANY youngsters are swotting just now for exams. And many parents are worried how they will do. Too worried sometimes.

You see, I've been enjoying a book about the life of Albert Einstein, possibly the most brilliant physicist of this century.

Einstein's father went to see his son's headmaster and asked his advice on what sort of a career young Einstein should aim for.

The headmaster said, " It doesn't matter what he does, he'll never make a success of anything."

THE FRIENDSHIP BOOK

SATURDAY—JANUARY 18.

I DIDN'T see her very much,
But Mrs Grey was kind.
She lived next door, and listened if
I'd something on my mind.
She lent me this, she lent me that;
Sometimes she'd shop for me;
And now and then we'd have a chat
Or share a cup of tea.
It wasn't till she'd moved away
I really missed our Mrs Grey!

SUNDAY—JANUARY 19.

HE that is faithful in that which is least, is faithful also in much.

MONDAY—JANUARY 20.

ELLA WHEELER WILCOX'S poems cheered and encouraged millions.

Her brave outlook on life and her simple faith are needed perhaps even more now than during her lifetime because life is more complex than it used to be. Standards have been lowered, selfishness and carelessness lead to bitterness and disillusionment, and though there is more money, there is also more misery.

When summer is still quite far off, and cold weather and long, dark nights seem to exaggerate our troubles, we need all our courage and cheerfulness to help us through the winter till spring brings new life and hope.

Ella put it this way:

Talk happiness. The world is sad enough
Without your woe. No path is wholly rough.

I find this practical and challenging counsel.

THE TRICK

The books tell how to do it.
You grip your club just so . . .
But till you've found out for yourself
You never really know.

DAVID HOPE

IN MINIATURE

Small things give their own especial pleasure.
I sometimes thought that this was very odd.
I know now why we love this minor measure —
It lets us for a moment play at God!

DAVID HOPE

TUESDAY—JANUARY 21.

TWO famous writers of the last century, William Makepeace Thackeray and Charles Dickens, had a great admiration for each other.

But one day, the two had an argument, as friends sometimes do, became heated, and parted with angry words. When next they met, each pretended not to see the other. Not long afterwards, they came face to face, glared stonily, and marched on. Then Thackeray suddenly turned back, rushed up to Dickens, seized his hand, and exclaimed that he could not think bitterly of him any longer. Dickens, deeply moved, embraced him.

Within a few days, Thackeray died. How thankful Dickens was that they became good friends again "just in time."

If you have a quarrel, make it up as soon as ever you can — as much for your own sake, as for the other party.

WEDNESDAY—JANUARY 22.

I HEARD of an unusual bargain the other day. The popular Scottish singer, Bill McCue, was heading for Glasgow after a concert in Aberdeen when his car broke down. He phoned a garage and the owner, Mr Dan Campbell, went out to the breakdown himself. The car had to be towed to the garage and was fixed within a couple of hours.

When the singer asked for his bill, Dan Campbell had a brainwave. In return for the repair would Bill McCue entertain the old folk at Dan's village the first time he was passing that way? Bill was delighted to accept the challenge. And that is how eighty members of Meigle Golden Age Club came to be entertained by Bill McCue, free of charge, one Tuesday afternoon. And how they enjoyed it!

THURSDAY—JANUARY 23.

ONE of the most striking Christmas cards we have received came from Canada. In a shining black panel on the front is a hole about the size of a penny ; and if you open the card a little you see a space photograph of the world partly lit by sunshine, and it floats in utter and complete blackness. There are six words in yellow print, from the Book of Job : He hangeth the earth upon nothing.

Whatever is happening to religion these days, one is driven to the conclusion that beyond the skill and knowledge of men is something infinitely mysterious which created and which controls this universe and the unfathomed wonder of life. We are presumptuous indeed if we dare to think there is no God.

FRIDAY—JANUARY 24.

I HAVE a " sunshine " memory of walking with my father along a country lane in the Cheviots. I had never re-visited this spot until last summer and was overjoyed to find the sun shining again.

Miraculously, nothing had changed except that in my childish memory there was a little stream that flowed by the side of the road and along its edges I remembered a profusion of yellow mimulus and blue forget-me-nots. I walked over to where I had remembered it and, getting down on my knees, I parted the grass and found that what, to a child's eye, had been a stream, was merely a small trickle of water, hidden by long grasses. The mimulus and forget-me-nots were still there.

Perhaps it would do us all a bit of good to get down on our knees more often and see things, again, through the eyes of a child.

SATURDAY—JANUARY 25.

GOING to work on winter mornings
Doesn't strike me as a joke.
Chilly winds to make you shiver,
Ice, or maybe just a soak.
Going to work on winter mornings
Isn't funny, you'll agree,
But could anything be better
Than returning home for tea?

SUNDAY—JANUARY 26.

FOR He hath said, I will never leave thee, nor forsake thee.

MONDAY—JANUARY 27.

FOR ten days Francis Gay was very sorry for himself.

He was fit as could be when he went to bed one evening, and no sooner was he warm and snug and ready to sleep than his left elbow began to ache. Then his shoulder started playing up, and all his left side felt as if it weighed ten tons!

The Lady of the House did what she could. But I had little sleep, and for the next few days and nights I was, as I repeat, sorry for myself, and suffered quite a lot from what, I'm told, was a touch of neuritis.

I'm thankful to say all's now right as rain, but while I suffered there was just no escape from torture. So I think I can sympathise a little more with those who suffer constantly and am more aware than I have ever been how impossible it is to describe a pain, and how mighty relieved one is when at last it eases.

Oh, what joy, what unbelievable joy!

A

TUESDAY—JANUARY 28.

I HEARD not long ago about a young man, brought up in a Methodist home, who had felt a call to enter the ministry.

But suddenly, as the preaching of his first sermon drew near, he got cold feet. In a sudden panic, he visited his grandfather. "Grandad," he said, "I'm due to conduct a service in a country chapel a week on Sunday. Whatever shall I tell the folk?"

The older man smiled. "Just tell them that God loves them," he said earnestly, "and that if they love God, and trust Him, all will be well."

It sounded too simple and the young man went away deeply despairing. But he began his sermon in the chapel with these words: "And now I'm going to tell you two things. First: What God has done for my grandfather; and second: What I believe God will do for me if I love and trust Him."

I understand that young man's first sermon was deeply moving and more than one listener came up to thank him for it.

WEDNESDAY—JANUARY 29.

"ELEVEN, 15, where's No. 13?" I asked the Lady of the House. She smiled. "There isn't one. You see, the people there are superstitious."

"Ah, yes," said I, smugly, "that's triskaideka-phobia." I had discovered only that morning the meaning of the word was "fear of the number 13."

Isn't it odd that, even in these days when everybody is so anxious to be "mod," the past is still with us—fear of 13, knives crossed on the dinner table, three sneezes, and so on.

We still haven't escaped from the Dark Ages, it seems.

THURSDAY—JANUARY 30.

SOME years ago I heard from an American friend about a schoolgirl of ten whose most treasured possession was a cameo brooch. It was the only piece of jewellery she had ever possessed.

One Sunday in church the pastor spoke about the starving victims of famine in India, and the congregation were asked to promise a gift to be handed in after three months. Mary pledged to give seventy-five dollars, and she hadn't a cent!

She tried hard to save money doing small jobs for neighbours, but when there was no more than a week left for the gift to be handed in, she had saved only 25 dollars. For a long time she struggled within herself, and at last went to the drug store and asked how much she could get for her beloved brooch.

"Well," murmured the man there, "this cameo brooch is the worse for wear, but I could maybe give you fifty dollars!"

So Mary sold the brooch, and, as promised, handed in her gift of seventy-five dollars.

The odd thing is that she was intensely happy —unbelievably so; and never has she regretted the sacrifice she made. In a life of over 97 years she has smiled along serenely . . . as most folk do if they have a loving heart and think more about others than about themselves!

FRIDAY—JANUARY 31.

THINGS aren't going well just now,
The months ahead look bleak;
The news, it seems, gets worse and worse
With every passing week.
And yet today, amid the gloom,
I found my first snowdrop in bloom!

FEBRUARY

I LIKE this Chinese legend because it reminds us of a truth we are in danger of forgetting.

Some hundreds of years ago, when the inhabitants of Pekin were collecting money to pay for a copper image of Buddah, a nun stood near the South Gate, collecting gifts and registering the names of donors. One morning a poor old man asked why she stood there, and the nun explained. " Ah," said the man, " this is all I have. Take it." Then he handed in a coin worth less than the old farthing in British currency.

The time came when the fashioning of the figure began. Tons of copper were thrown into the huge furnace, but though the heat was even greater than usual, the immense mass of metal did not melt. Puzzled, the chief coppersmith made inquiries, and eventually the nun confessed that she had not handed in the tiny Chinese copper coin because it was of such small worth. Pressed to hand the coin over, she did so, and it was thrown into the furnace. Immediately the copper began to melt, and soon the image was complete.

Only a legend, of course, but the message is clear. There is nothing really insignificant in this world, and even great undertakings demand the honest, careful work of people who think they don't count.

MAN doth not live by bread alone, but by every word that proceedeth out of the mouth of the Lord doth man live.

MONDAY—FEBRUARY 3.

AS a friend of mine was talking to a gamekeeper one evening, he heard the cry of wild geese overhead, settling for a night's rest before their remarkable journey to the Far North to nest amid the lonely wastes of the Arctic Circle.

My friend looked up and remarked on how the great V formation seems constantly to change shape, almost as if it is straggling.

The keeper said the reason the skein is always changing is that, as one leader tires, another comes forward to take its place, and the old leader falls into the slipstream of the new one. So it goes on right down the line, the stronger birds instinctively helping the weaker. It is in this way that these great skeins of geese can battle their way through the storms that threaten our most powerful ships, and fly a thousand miles to their nesting place.

As he heard the geese disappear, my friend could not help but think of it as a parable for all mankind.

TUESDAY—FEBRUARY 4.

MY birthday is not for some time yet, but the Lady of the House asked me the other day if there was anything I'd like as a present. I mentioned something I've wanted for years, but as I felt it was a bit too dear, I suggested I might pay for part of it myself.

She thought for a moment. " Well," she said tentatively, " it isn't really what I had in mind for you." I smiled patiently. " Right," I replied, " tell me what you thought about, and I'll tell you if I'd prefer it."

" Oh, no," she explained promptly. " It wouldn't be a surprise then!"

Wondrous indeed are a woman's ways!

THE FRIENDSHIP BOOK

MISS EDNA FINLAY passes on the story of the clergyman whose car gave a small boy a bump.

It was the boy's own fault, though thankfully he wasn't hurt in the least. But, for all that, the clergyman called at the boy's home to make his apologies.

As there was no one in, however, the clergyman dropped his card through the letterbox, with a brief note beginning, " Sorry I missed you . . ."

THE Lady of the House was reading a newspaper when she held up a picture of the Queen Mother.

She said she'd noticed the Queen Mother is hardly ever seen without her necklace—four strands of pearls—whatever else she may be wearing. They are there on great occasions, such as the Queen's Coronation. She wears them when she visits an old people's home or a hospital. They are round her neck when she launches a ship, addresses a university, even when she is out fishing or up on the moors. " I'm sure it must mean something very special to her," said my wife.

Well, she is right. The necklace was a wedding gift from King George in 1923. Though she possesses jewellery that is far more valuable, it has been her most precious possession for over 50 years. Hardly a day has passed without her wearing the pearls, and since the King's death in 1952, they have come to mean even more.

That is the secret of the Queen Mother's necklace, and every woman who treasures the keepsake of a loved one will understand what it means.

THE FRIENDSHIP BOOK

I'D like to be much better off—
But not too rich I think.
For I have noticed wealthy folk
Are seldom in the pink.
Somehow they miss a lot of thrills
Which come to you and me—
A modest house is cosier than
A stately home can be.
Wage-earning folk who pay the rent
Are rich, if only they're content.

SATURDAY—FEBRUARY 8.

DO you know where your wife keeps the clothes pegs ?

I don't, but one Monday I chanced to see Jean and Jim Livingstone, of 59 Loch Ryan Street, Stranraer, on that TV programme called " Mr and Mrs." A smiling couple who, after thirty years of marriage, still seemed ideally happy. Jim was able to say correctly, how often Jean washes her kitchen floor, how she'd view a new hair-do, and where she keeps her clothes pegs. Jean knew what kind of bacon Jim likes best, what he'd do if he'd to go out while she wasn't at home, and how often he checked his weight. Also all correct. It brought them a jackpot prize of £250.

And it made me think. If I'd been asked the same kind of questions about the Lady of the House would I have known the answers ? If not, why not ? Indeed, it struck me that perhaps the secret of Jim and Jean's obvious happiness is that each is aware of every little detail of the other's day to day life, and shares every aspect of it.

Togetherness is the modern word for it, I think— and that's worth more than any jackpot !

THE FRIENDSHIP BOOK

THE Son of man came not to be ministered unto, but to minister, and to give his life a ransom for many.

SOME years ago, there was a crisis in a certain Glasgow office. The man who looked after the welfare of the deaf had been called to another post. No one could be found to succeed him.

Then someone remembered a young man who worked in Paisley. His mother and father were deaf and dumb. He could speak to the deaf in sign language. Why not ask him?

At first he wasn't sure. But he decided to give up his job and take the plunge.

Today he is still devoting his life to the welfare of the deaf and dumb. His name—the Rev. J. Stewart Lochrie, whose TV appearances have moved thousands, and whose tireless work has meant so much to so many. He helps young men at interviews for jobs. He helps parents to cope with deaf children. He visits hospitals and homes, and is the only light in many a lonely, silent life.

What seemed a disaster turned out to be a blessing —and, as Mr Lochrie will tell you, to none more than himself.

IF ever you've a little thought,
*   An urge to do a friendly act,*
Don't stifle it, but go ahead
*   And turn that impulse into fact.*
A kindness done to someone sad
Will make your own heart twice as glad.

WEDNESDAY—FEBRUARY 12.

MY old friend, Jack McKibbin, tells the story of a recent christening.

At the service, the minister was waxing eloquent about the road stretched out before the child who lay cradled in his arms.

"Think of the future before him," he said. "He may become a leader of industry, a sea captain, a clergyman like myself, or a gifted teacher on whom hundreds of boys may model themselves."

Then, turning to the parents, he asked grandly, "What name do you give this child?"

Timidly, the baby's mother replied, "Amanda Jane . . ."

THURSDAY—FEBRUARY 13.

SHOULD you be looking for an angel—you may find one disguised as a housewife, carrying a shopping basket and a parcel of laundry.

Mrs Margaret Thomson, of 24 Stirling Road, Callander, has been taking the bus to Dunblane every Thursday for eighteen years. There she goes to 2 Golfhill, the home of her 89-year-old widowed father.

First she rolls up her sleeves, gets out the scrubbing brush and washes the outside passage. Out comes the duster and she makes the house shipshape. After tea, George gets out his melodeon and Margaret sits down to listen to an old favourite or two. They chat and she tells him all the family news. Then Margaret goes home to her husband and family in Callander.

Now I know how much these weekly visits mean to George. And I take this opportunity to doff my hat to those other angels with shopping bags we may daily pass unawares.

FRIDAY—FEBRUARY 14.

H OWEVER dark your night may be,
However deep your pain,
There always comes a dawn, when you
Can see some light again —
A peace you might have never had
If you had never been so sad.

SATURDAY—FEBRUARY 15.

A FEW days ago I picked up a letter with my mother's signature. It was one she had written to a young friend, Jessie. When my mother died, Jessie sent me the letter " for keeps."

Jessie was a charming lassie gifted with a remarkable soprano voice. She was also a wonderful musician. When she was in her early twenties someone tried to persuade Jessie to become an opera singer, and offered to pay all her expenses, but she very graciously and also firmly refused. Local folk said Jessie turned down opportunities to sing in London, Italy, the U.S.A., and so on. But Jessie sang because she enjoyed singing. She sang without charging a fee. For miles round her home she was the star turn of concerts in village halls and at church services. She married well, had two children, and though she died comparatively young she had a wonderfully happy life.

The last sentence in my mother's letter to Jessie was : " We are all so proud of you, my dear . . . and so nice of you to sing for just ordinary folk such as we are."

SUNDAY—FEBRUARY 16.

THOU shalt worship the Lord thy God, and him only shalt thou serve.

Monday—February 17.

A FRIEND in Australia tells me about 800 soldiers in a camp near Sydney.

Every morning, they were aroused at 6.30 by a bugler sounding Reveille. But one morning, every man in the camp tumbled out of bed to the sound of the bugle—and found it was only 4 a.m.

What happened? In that part of Australia are birds which are wonderful mimics. They'd heard the bugle—and soon they were sounding a reveille at 4 a.m. every morning. Something had to be done.

The camp commander ordered the bugler to stand down—and after that his men were awakened to the sound of bagpipes!

The birds, says my friend, tried for some time to mimic the pipes—then gave up in disgust and flew off to pastures new.

Tuesday—February 18.

NOW and again a letter drops through my box from a businessman whose name I know, but who prefers to be known as J. M. R.

In his leisure moments, he enjoys nothing more than jotting down verses—lines with a smile, or a thought, or a bit of his own quiet philosophy. And sometimes these find their way to me.

His latest offering is, in its way, a recipe for life. I'm sure you will enjoy it:

Whatever be your mood—don't be rude.
Whatever comes your way—please be gay.
Whatever cares you know—let them go.
Whatever path you choose—quit the blues.
Whatever be the test—do your best.
Whatever be the strain—don't complain.
To make life more worthwhile—whatever
   happens, SMILE!

THE FRIENDSHIP BOOK

YOU long for bairns, but still have none?
In secret you may weep?
You ache to have a bairn to love —
The hurt goes very deep?
But there is something you can do —
Be " mother " to a bairn or two!

WHILE visiting a friend recently I glanced at one of his bookshelves, noting among academic works a book by Ruby M. Ayres—a light romance called " Some Day."

Times have changed vastly since " Some Day " was published in 1935, but I found a message in it for folk who are finding the going hard today. One of her characters says :

" I used to look at that milestone, and realise there was only another mile to go before I reached the place which was to be the place where I realised my life's ambition. That's how I should like you to look at all the bad patches, Denise—just that they bring you a little nearer to the good things."

It's true, isn't it ?

WHILE on holiday at Leeds, writes Miss A. Sumner, I noticed this inscription on the sundial in a park there :

He stands alone amid the flowers
And only counts the sunny hours.
Dull days for him do not exist,
The brazen-faced old optimist.

Maybe we ought to be like that sundial and count only the sunny hours.

SATURDAY—FEBRUARY 22.

"**R**OBERT GRAHAM, he gave the money for the building of this bridge. By the Grace of God, he served his Generation."

That inscription is written upon the time-stained walls of a wayside bridge in a remote part of the North, near Bewcastle, Cumberland.

The old bridge is a pleasant place to cross in summer. In winter, when the flood-waters rush upon their headstrong journey to the distant sea, it still safely bears the traveller on to his journey's end.

If we could build a bridge—of kindness or friendship that would aid a fellow-traveller on his way in life, may it also be recorded of us that we "served our Generation."

SUNDAY—FEBRUARY 23.

HE that hath two coats, let him impart to him that hath none, and he that hath meat, let him do likewise.

MONDAY—FEBRUARY 24.

NOT long ago I attended the funeral of a good friend, a professional man who, in quiet ways known only to a few, had helped a multitude.

As I walked away from the graveside, someone near me commented cynically, "Yes, it seems we're all good folk when we're dead."

I hope my friend's family did not overhear that remark. But it reminded me of advice given to me when I was quite young.

It was simply this. Before you say a word about another, ask yourself three questions :

Is it true ? Is it kind ? Is it necessary ?

If the answer is "No," then say nothing.

TUESDAY—FEBRUARY 25.

IN a narrow lane off Perth Road, Dundee, stood St Mary's mothercraft centre. From all over Scotland, came young mothers who couldn't cope.

Some never had a mother of their own to learn from. Others had husbands who were wasters. Name any problem and sooner or later you'd find it at St Mary's. Yet today, many of these mothers now live happy, decent lives, thanks to the woman who was matron there for twelve years—Miss Ellen Gardiner.

Miss Gardiner herself had her cross to bear. Her health was never good. Ever since I have known her, her back has been encased in a steel brace and she has been in constant pain. As a child she had a happy home and this helped her to keep going.

St Mary's is closed now. But Miss Gardiner was telling me with quiet pride of an honour that means more to her than words can say. In her early years there, a family named Kerr came from Glasgow for a spell. One of them was a little girl of eight or nine. She never forgot Miss Gardiner when she went home.

Now, grown-up and married, she has just had her first baby girl—and she has called her Ellen Gardiner, after the woman who, many years ago, taught her the untold blessing of a happy home.

WEDNESDAY—FEBRUARY 26.

THE table cleared, the dishes washed,
*   The children in their cots;*
The fire aglow — just me and Joe
*   Together with our thoughts.*
Things may be hard, the future grey —
But oh, what wealth is ours today!

MORNING MILKING

With tender grass on which to feed
Morag is quite content.
She gives us all the milk we need
And thinks the days well spent.

DAVID HOPE

B

A HOUSE WITH A VIEW

Folk boast of their gardens and what they grow.
We smile and say nothing because we know

However exotic their plants and flowers,
They don't have a waterfall like ours!

DAVID HOPE

LUNCH TIME

Peace can still be found in quiet places
Remote from motorways,
Where men can cultivate the ancient graces
And pass contented days.

DAVID HOPE

THE FRIENDSHIP BOOK

IN the silence of the night and in the presence of " death's bright angel " was born one of the best-loved of all songs.

For three weeks Arthur Sullivan—later Sir Arthur—had spent every night at the bedside of his only brother, whom he loved dearly. On that last vigil, when the patient was evidently sinking, Arthur was tired, distressed, unable to watch and unable to leave the room before the end came.

Wandering between window and door, he picked up a book and turned its pages idly. He found himself reading some verses written by Adelaide Ann Proctor, and suddenly a few lines inspired a tune. There and then the musician set down on paper a few bars ; and as the dawn came the theme of " The Lost Chord " was composed.

Strange that out of pain and sorrow and heart-break should come the song that has been sung round the world, and has touched the hearts of millions.

IDLY turning the pages of a dictionary a few days ago, I found a bit of Latin.

I was never much good at Latin at school, and I have forgotten most of the bit I learnt. But you know, the Latin writers who died many centuries ago could say a lot in very few words. It's just about a lost art today.

So, I paused to read four words written by Seneca over 1900 years ago : " Si vis amari, ama." My little Latin enabled me to translate this into seven words—words that go deep and could change your whole way of life. *If you wish to be loved, love.*

Neat, surely ? And how true !

MARCH

SATURDAY—MARCH 1.

THE roof was leaking and, after various delays, the slater had arrived. The housewife watched, somewhat impatiently, as a tough-looking youth removed the slates, his transistor blaring in his pocket.

Suddenly he switched off and shouted to the woman below.

" Here, Missis, there's a nest in there !"

" A nest ?"

" Aye. With four young chicks. I'll not be able to get in to work with them there. Couldn't you put up with them a bit longer ?"

" Well . . ."

" No, I couldn't do it, Missis. Give them another coupla weeks an' I'll come back. They'll be flyin' by then." Gently he replaced the tiles, leaving enough room for air.

" You know what it's like," he apologised, switched on the transistor deafeningly, and went back to report to his boss.

When he had gone, the mother bird nipped in to see that all was well. For some reason, everyone, including the woman with the leak in her ceiling, felt warmed and happy ; and as if to reward a good deed, the rain stayed off till the fledglings had flown and the roof was mended.

Appearances can be deceptive sometimes.

SUNDAY—MARCH 2.

AND this is the confidence that we have in Him, that if we ask anything according to His will, He heareth us.

THE FRIENDSHIP BOOK

MONDAY—MARCH 3.

HOW often the frankness of children may cut dignity down to size.

A dignified Bishop of London told how he was sitting in Hyde Park and, as he stumbled in rising from his seat, a small child rushed forward to help him. Pleased, he exaggerated his difficulty and complimented the child, " That was kind of you."

" Oh," she replied, " it's all right. I've often helped Daddy when he has been as drunk as you are."

TUESDAY—MARCH 4.

MAGGIE and Will have been married more than 50 years.

Like most husbands, Will is given to reading out snippets from the newspapers, expecting his wife to be interested. Maggie has perfected the art of the gentle reply, which keeps Will happy, while scarcely interrupting her own thoughts.

The other day Will's eyebrows went up as he was looking at his morning paper. " It says here," he said, " that a man is run over in New York every half-hour."

" Goodness," said Maggie, " you'd think by this time he'd have learned to look out when he's crossing the road !"

Will simply nodded in agreement !

WEDNESDAY—MARCH 5.

*W*HEN *wet the street and cold your feet,*
*   It's sometimes hard to do.*
I know that if it's hard for me
*   It must be hard for you!*
But if in cheerless weather we
Can smile a smile — how nice to see!

B

THURSDAY—MARCH 6.

AT Castle Asconate on Lake Como a visitor was delighted to see the gardens in perfect order. "How often does the owner come?" he asked a gardener. "It is twelve years since he was here last," was the reply, adding, "We get our orders from an agent in Milan."

"But you keep everything as if your master was coming tomorrow," complimented the visitor.

The old gardener's eyes glistened as he replied, "Maybe today, sir. Maybe today."

FRIDAY—MARCH 7.

DURING the First World War the Rev. "Tubby" Clayton was the genial host as well as chaplain at Talbot House in Poperinghe, Flanders. It was a soldiers' home with a difference. Over the entrance was the sign: "Abandon Rank All Ye Who Enter Here." Inside was the notice, "Write your names in the visitors' book. How else can we trace our spoons or return your umbrella?"

The cheerful atmosphere was continued in the canteen with, "Wash your own cup and saucer. This is the maid's night out," and in the writing-room, "If you are accustomed to spit on the floor at home you are permitted to spit here." "These pens are to be used for writing and not as darts." "No swearing *aloud*."

The serviceman, introduced thus to the atmosphere, made his way to the chapel in the attic where he met "Tubby" ready to give help and encouragement or to join in the nightly prayers.

The founder is dead now, but the movement lives on in Toc H, where old comrades are remembered and the spirit of service is inspired.

THE FRIENDSHIP BOOK

WHEN very sorry for yourself,
Don't sit around and sigh.
Don't ask why you'll have chores to do
Until the day you die.
Just set to work and get them done —
You'll find life still holds lots of fun!

SUNDAY—MARCH 9.

TODAY many mums will be enjoying breakfast in bed and other favours. Why?

Because it's Mother's Day. Mothering Sunday in the Church of England calendar is of unknown origin, but Mother's Day in the United States was started by Anna Jarvis on May 9, 1907. Her mother had died 12 months previously and she persuaded relatives and friends to honour this day. The idea spread, and in 1914 President Woodrow Wilson signed a resolution calling for the observance of Mother's Day on the second Sunday in May.

How thrilled Miss Jarvis would have been to know how her idea had escalated!

MONDAY—MARCH 10.

A WOMAN, notorious as a malicious gossip, went to Confession and was told as a penance to walk a mile plucking feathers off a hen all the way. She did so and, on her return, was told, "Now retrace your steps and gather up all the feathers." "But, that's impossible, they are all blown away by the wind," she replied.

Then it was pointed out to her how her careless conversation could spread, and cause unnecessary pain to her neighbours. "Boys flying kites can draw them in at will. You can't do that with words."

TUESDAY—MARCH 11.

SOME time ago Miss Harper, of Milton Road, Edinburgh, had two girls staying with her for a holiday. They went to the Zoo one day, and on entering the park were faced with a large notice-board directing visitors to the various animal houses.

They stood looking for a moment, then Jean said, " Which animal do you think we should go and see first ? " So Helen studied the board.

" I think we should go to see these first, as they're almost extinct," she said, with a twinkle in her eye, pointing to the word " Gentlemen."

WEDNESDAY—MARCH 12.

MAKE little of your miseries —
Each pinprick, hurt or loss.
Make much of any bit of luck
You chance to come across.
You'll find, as you go gaily through,
Life's mostly rather kind to you!

THURSDAY—MARCH 13.

LOTS of senior citizens coming up to their eighties feel they have outlived their usefulness, but to prove how wrong they can be, look at Mr Ivie Easton, of St Monans in Fife.

Mr Easton still repairs watches and clocks. He is also a keen photographer. In one way his age is actually an advantage for, from his own memory and by being able to produce old records, dating back to 1870, of events in the burgh, he can give the last word in disputes between locals.

I think you will agree he is a wonderful example to people who think life stops when you begin to draw your pension.

FRIDAY—MARCH 14.

ONE of our young friends has a boy friend called Bill, who is a garage mechanic.

She took him home one Sunday, but her dad disapproved of his long hair. He told her, "Don't bring that long-haired lout here again!"

When out alone with the car her dad had a breakdown miles from home. He phoned the nearest garage, and an employee arrived and towed his car home.

As he came into the house with the mechanic, he said, "Give this young man the supper he well deserves."

Bill and our friend exchanged glances, then burst out laughing.

Dad had brought home the "long-haired lout" and has now accepted him as his future son-in-law.

SATURDAY—MARCH 15.

ALL the world knows the story of Greyfriars' Bobby, the dog who kept faithful watch over his master's grave for fifteen years.

But there is a side effect of the loyalty that may not be so well known. In the high tenements surrounding the graveyard the inhabitants grew so interested in watching the dog coming and going on sentinel guard that, to see him better, they cleaned the begrimed windows of their homes and, as the light grew stronger in the spring, it showed up the dusty and sometimes dirtier interiors.

It may seem strange to think of a dog being an incentive to spring cleaning, but "Bobby" did more for the people than he could have known. How often affection for an animal does brighten our homes and our hearts.

SUNDAY—MARCH 16.

CHILDREN, how hard is it for them that trust in riches to enter into the kingdom of God!

MONDAY—MARCH 17.

MISS MACKAY is 22, dark, attractive, and a teacher in charge of more than 30 nine-year-olds.

She was giving them a grammar lesson the other day, and initiating them into the dangers and mysteries of the double negative. To illustrate her point she wrote a sentence on the blackboard:

"*I didn't have no fun at the party last night.*"

Then she turned to the class. "Now," she smiled, "how do I put that right?"

Immediately, up piped a voice from the front row—"Get yourself a boy friend, miss!"

TUESDAY—MARCH 18.

IN a hut in Dunblane, Perthshire, an unusual reunion takes place each year. Only sixteen people are eligible, and they come from as far afield as Devon and Aberdeen. They were all members of a Rover Scout crew formed before the war and kept in touch over the years by the one member who could not join the Armed Forces because he was confined to a wheelchair. He was John Davidson. Separated from his friends, he began a news-letter and sent it every month to fellow Rovers. After the war ended, he came up with the idea of a reunion.

Though it is eighteen years since John died, his old comrades still remember him and it is really in his memory that the remaining members of the crew meet in the same hut once a year.

THE LESSON

An old, old doorway, but the stone
Still teaches us today
That now, as then in times long gone,
Fair dealing must hold sway.

C   DAVID HOPE

WHAT'S GOING ON?

The world's an interesting place
With sights and sounds galore.
It's quite exciting just to stand
And watch it from our door.

DAVID HOPE

WEDNESDAY—MARCH 19.

NOT long ago John McGhie and his wife, of Perth, went off to Sutherland for a few days' holiday. They planned to go to a house they had visited before, for bed and breakfast. When they arrived, they were welcomed with a smile.

They explained they'd like to stay over the week-end. To their surprise, a look of doubt crossed the face of the kindly Highland body whose home it was and she explained that she didn't usually keep people over the Sabbath. It was against her principles to do business on Sundays. Of course, Mr and Mrs McGhie were disappointed—but they respected her beliefs. " Don't worry," they said. " We'll make other arrangements."

Then their landlady smiled, and shook her head. " No you won't," she said. " You're welcome to stay as my guests. I won't charge you for your beds, or for your meals—you'll be here as friends."

Now, maybe you think the Highland Sabbath is a bit much in this modern age. But whatever you believe, doesn't it challenge you to hear of someone ready to stick to the principles she holds, even when she stands to lose by doing so ?

THURSDAY—MARCH 20.

OUR old friend, Mary Atherton, of Windsor, Ontario, had not been keeping too well. But still come cheery letters and snippets which she thinks I may be interested in. Among the thoughts which Mary sent, I found two lines in which there's something for most of us.

Said Mary : It's no use putting your hand to the plough unless you're prepared to push it.

An ounce of effort, remember, is worth a ton of good intentions !

THE FRIENDSHIP BOOK

PROFESSOR VAN DUSEN wrote a book after the Second World War, "They Found the Church There." I am glad to take one extract from it, the letter of an American airman which shows how God's purposes may work out.

"Please send ten dollars from my bank account to the missionary society working here. If I had parachuted down from a burning plane fifty years ago I would have been boiled and eaten. Instead, I have been treated with the utmost kindness and consideration by the amazing Christian community on this island."

An almost unknown isle in the Phillipines, but the story of missionary enterprise can be repeated in a host of places.

A YOUNG man last century was suffering from tuberculosis. He was sent to a sanatorium, and the chief medical officer asked the patient if his home doctor had given him any advice.

"He says I am to have plenty of fresh air and fresh eggs, and I am to read books by Robert Louis Stevenson every day," was the reply.

"Your doctor," said the chief medical officer, "obviously knows his job, and of the three medicines he prescribes the last is probably the best."

Robert Louis Stevenson suffered from ill-health all his days. But he wrote countless books (including "Treasure Island"), and all through life refused to allow his ill-health to frighten him or prevent him keeping on with his pen. He was born in Edinburgh, and died, before he was 45, in the South Sea island which had become his home—a gallant fighter to the end.

SUNDAY—MARCH 23.

FOR the good that I would, I do not; but the evil which I would not, that I do.

MONDAY—MARCH 24.

SOME years ago a group of folk in a small American town wished to build a youth club for their youngsters.

After examining the problem for a long time they reluctantly came to the conclusion that it would cost more than they could possibly afford

One morning Charlie, a schoolboy, knocked on the door of the group's leader. " Sir," he said, " here's half a dozen bricks from the bottom of our yard. I've wheeled 'em over in my barrow, and if you want 'em you can have 'em."

Charlie's six bricks were not enough, of course. But they were a challenge. With new zeal and fresh determination the group began, continued and finished what at one time they " knew " simply couldn't be done !

I leave you with the message.

TUESDAY—MARCH 25.

CHARLES SPURGEON was famous as a preacher and renowned for his ready wit. Often his congregation chuckled " with one vast smile."

Once he was asked by a congregation if he could get them a minister big enough to fill their church.

" You fill the church," he replied, " and I'll get you a minister big enough to fill the pulpit."

He loved to twit his congregation into a good humour, once saying, " If you are Christians, smile. But, if not, your ordinary faces will do."

After that, who could remain glum !

THE FRIENDSHIP BOOK

HOW rich are you?

Most Saturdays a friend of mine used to take a grand old man of Scottish football to a game somewhere—Jimmy Brownlie, the son of a Blantyre miner, who went on to become a brilliant goalkeeper, and was capped for Scotland 16 times. Jimmy died at 88, as shrewd a judge of men and of football as he ever was.

Not long before, my friend stopped his car outside the house in Dundee, where Jimmy lived. The old man had thoroughly enjoyed the match. Before he got out, he turned to my friend. "You know," he said seriously, "I pray for you every night." The man beside him was deeply touched. "Do you, Jimmy?" he said. "Aye," the old man went on. "First I pray for my family. Then my grandchildren. And then I pray for a' ma friends . . ." Then, with the hint of a smile, asked, "Am I daft?"

"No, Jimmy, you're not daft," replied my friend—and he meant it. Indeed, it is one of the finest tributes any man can pay another. And surely it is significant that, at the end of a life so full as Jimmy's, the things which meant most to him were not the fame and the golden memories of days gone by, but his family, the bairns and the company of his friends.

How truly rich is a man who possesses these!

YOUR pictures down, your carpets up —
A lot of fuss and scrubbing,
Much soap and water all day long —
And arm-ache after rubbing!
One day, when brightly shines the sun,
How glad you'll be spring cleaning's done!

FRIDAY—MARCH 28.

A TEACHER'S job gets no easier these days—and TV doesn't help !

Even the commercial breaks have their hazards. A Belfast teacher had been telling her class of seven-year-olds something about the Middle East war, and mentioned Damascus once or twice.

When she finished, she pointed at one wee girl who obviously hadn't been paying attention. " Judith," she said severely, " can you tell me anything about Damascus ?"

" Yes, Miss," replied Judith with a confident smile. " It kills 99 per cent of all known germs !"

SATURDAY—MARCH 29.

IRENE GRANT, an American friend in California, sends me a story about a tree.

It was a giant redwood. For well over 400 years it stood proudly aloof. Rain and wind beat upon that tree ; periods of drought dried up its sap ; they say it was struck by lightning at least a dozen times, and I am told that even a powerful earthquake failed to dislodge it. But one day not long ago the redwood fell, crashing without warning amid the thunder of its own making.

The cause ? Simply that somewhere below the bark, tiny beetles had riddled the timber, thus accomplishing in secret what tempest, drought, lightning and earthquake had failed to do in over four centuries.

Some would have you believe that little lies, little dishonesties, small ways in which we are tempted to do or give less than our best are unimportant and of no account.

If you accept that, remember the parable of the giant redwood tree — and beware the little beetles !

SUNDAY—MARCH 30.

FOR as the heaven is high above the earth, so great is His mercy toward them that fear Him.

MONDAY—MARCH 31.

YOU don't expect to buy tea in a draper's shop, do you?

But you can — in Jarvis the drapers in Forfar. This is how it came about.

In 1874, a young man called William Jarvis set out, with a suitcase in one hand and a pack over his back, going round the villages, cottar houses and farms of Angus selling everything he could carry from tea to ribbons. It wasn't an easy life, but he persevered. When he didn't have what a customer wanted he'd promise to bring it on his next round—and he never failed to keep his promise.

In time he prospered and he was able to buy a shop in Forfar. He set out to build a drapery business, but so many customers kept asking for the tea he'd sold on his rounds, he decided to sell it, too, for, in a way, it had been the special blend of tea that had been the backbone of his early business.

The shop in Castle Street, Forfar, is still a family business, run by William's son, Charles. Like his father, he, too, sells shirts, trousers, socks, ties, &c. — and, of course, tea. And, Charles says, as long as there's a Jarvis in Castle Street, there will be tea on the counter.

What appeals to me is not just the story of a draper who surprisingly sells tea. But that the Jarvises are proud, and rightly so, of their beginnings, humble though these were.

APRIL

TUESDAY—APRIL 1.

EASTER has come and gone. What does it mean to you?

David Orrock was in his early 20's when he joined up, was captured by the Japanese, and put to work on the Burma railway.

For more than a year he laboured there. Every mile of the track that pushed its way through the jungle was marked by the rough graves of those who did not survive.

One night, the guards halted the prisoners outside the camp. Cholera raged inside. They were ordered to sleep in the open. All through the night, the bodies of victims were carried past. Early next day, the tattered band of prisoners was marched off again.

As they passed the graves of those who had died, David saw, towering above them, a stark wooden cross. Somehow for David it brought home the meaning of Easter as never before. Even amid the tragedy it symbolised triumph—and that moment of realisation changed David's life.

When he came home, he became a minister And I am sure that each Easter, as he stands in his pulpit, he will recall the message of that cross.

WEDNESDAY—APRIL 2.

*W*HEN *everything is wrong as wrong,*
And you yourself are wrong side out;
When folk or things just make you want
To weep alone, or loudly shout.
For goodness sake count up to ten,
Then grit your teeth and start again.

THE FRIENDSHIP BOOK

I KNOW a lady doctor who is cool, confident and very efficient. Her surgeries are invariably crowded, her days long and busy.

But recently I heard that after prescribing for one of her patients—a thin, tired mother of four—she said gently, " You and your husband going anywhere next Wednesday evening ? No ? I've two tickets here for the theatre. Could the two of you have a night out together ?"

The patient hesitated. " It's nice of you," she began. " But I'm afraid, if you don't mind . . ."

" No one to leave with the children ?"

" No one."

" O K. Look forward to that night out—I know just the person to baby-sit for you, Leave it to me."

So easy to be sorry for folk. Not so easy to do something about it !

PEARLS are among the most beautiful of all jewels.

Yet, curiously enough, this very loveliness is the result of suffering. For the beginning of a pearl is a sharp grain of sand which becomes buried in the folds of an oyster, and—like a speck of dust in your eye—causes such discomfort the oyster continually tries to cover it with calcium carbonate. In the end it turns the irritant into a smooth, roundish object—a pearl.

Here is a lesson for us all. Our pleasures are indeed to be enjoyed. But when vexation or pain or misfortune threaten to spoil our life it is for us to exercise restraint and courage and patience, thus making the best of the worst, and changing what might so easily spoil us into a pearl of great price.

THE FRIENDSHIP BOOK

YOU may not know this odd little tale about Rudyard Kipling, the famous writer who lived for many years in India and died in 1936.

One day, while visiting London zoo, he heard that a new elephant was slowly dying. It refused to eat anything, was giving no end of trouble and seemed unable to settle. The minute Kipling saw the animal he said, " Why, the beast is homesick !" Kipling went up to the elephant and began talking quietly to him in Hindustani. Gently, using all the words his owner in India would have been likely to use, he murmured, " Take it easy, old fellow."

To everybody's amazement the effect was magical. The elephant calmed down at once and became docile with his keepers.

It's the same with people, isn't it? Unless we show patience and understanding, we cannot expect to enter into the confidence of folk around us.

SUNDAY—APRIL 6.

I KNOW that my redeemer liveth, and that he shall stand at the latter day upon the earth.

MONDAY—APRIL 7.

I DIDN'T want to start the job,
But felt I really MUST.
My goodness, you would hardly think
There COULD be so much dust!
Well, I pitched in with half a grin,
I rubbed and scrubbed away;
I polished till my poor arms ached—
And kept on day by day.
Spring cleaning nearly drives me mad,
But when it's done, say, AM I GLAD!

TUESDAY—APRIL 8.

IT'S the little things that so often make a holiday, isn't it?

I'm thinking, for example, of crisp, smooth sheets to welcome you when you're pleasantly tired from a change of air. Or a neat, clean towel by the wash-basin.

And if you've been to Pitlochry recently, the chances are that sparkling fresh linen in your hotel or guest house comes from the local laundry where it is ironed by Mary Hudson. Yet for twenty years, Mary has been blind. It started so simply. A fall on an icy pavement, a knock on the head, and within weeks, Mary's sight had gone. Yet all day long, brisk and bright, she guides a big mechanical iron, smoothing, pressing, freshening, so that every piece of linen is a proud flag of her victory over adversity.

I hereby invite every holidaymaker to give her three hearty cheers.

WEDNESDAY—APRIL 9.

THE Lady of the House and I know a frail widow who is back home knowing she can never be well again, and that her days are running out.

But she is not perturbed. Indeed, she is thankful that her husband never lived to see her suffer ; thankful that her family is independent and doing nicely ; thankful that tablets make life at least tolerable ; thankful that she has time and opportunity still to do some of the things she had been meaning to do but didn't get done because she thought there was more time than there is . . .

When life presents us with an ultimatum, it's amazing what we can do, what we can endure calmly and confidently and even happily.

THURSDAY—APRIL 10.

THIS story, from Mrs Babs Henderson, began over thirty years ago, when her mother was widowed.

Mrs Henderson was two, and her sister twelve, and they didn't realise then how hard their mum struggled to give them a happy home. Indeed, she had only two treasures — two rings, which she planned to give her girls as tokens of remembrance when she was gone.

Alas, the rings went missing and, convinced they were gone for ever, she gave the girls another ring each instead of the ones she'd lost. But how sad she was they weren't the keepsakes she'd planned.

Then, one autumn, she took ill, and died not long afterwards. In the weeks that followed, the two sisters had the sad task of breaking up their mother's home — and that was when it happened.

Tucked away out of sight at the back of a drawer, under piles of linen, they found a little box. And there inside, gleaming gold, were the two treasured rings their mother thought she'd lost! It was a moment of mixed feelings — sadness the rings had been found just too late, and joy that their mum's dearest wish was fulfilled after all.

The rings will always be symbols of a love that never failed or faltered.

FRIDAY—APRIL 11.

THE world's a sorry place these days —
Disquieting and mad;
And most of us have troubles which
Are bound to make us sad.
But somehow every grief and care
Weighs less when spring is in the air!

SATURDAY—APRIL 12.

A LADY who is often in demand for public speaking was telling me about her experiences.

"I was terrified at first," she said. "When they rang me up I was just on the point of refusing, 'What on earth do you want me to talk about?' I asked; and the woman on the other end said, 'Oh, it really doesn't matter what you speak about so long as you come yourself.'"

It's the person who counts, after all.

SUNDAY—APRIL 13.

BE strong, and let your heart take courage, all ye that hope in the Lord.

MONDAY—APRIL 14.

FRIENDS of ours have just moved into a new house. The previous owner hadn't been well and the garden was in a state. Our friend is not keen on gardening, but eventually a start had to be made. The first evening passed very quickly. A man walking his dog introduced himself as a neighbour, and they chatted.

A little boy came in for his ball, and told my friend about his new puppy. A lady stopped her car, introduced herself and asked his wife to a coffee morning. The next night a passer-by told him all about the local bowling green, and the man across the road came over and offered some cuttings.

In short, his evenings in the garden became an introduction to his new neighbours. The job he'd been loth to tackle yielded up that rare plant, friendship.

Makes you think, doesn't it?

THE FRIENDSHIP BOOK

DO you look on the bright side of life?

Or do you see worries and pitfalls round every corner?

This letter was sent to me by a lady who, with her husband, made a bold decision.

"Twenty-five years ago we were told we couldn't have children. Our sky fell in. After a while we began to consider adoption. There were those who said to us — Are you wise? You've no idea how the child will turn out. Our reply was — Does anyone know how their own will turn out?

"We adopted a baby girl. Two years later we adopted a boy. No two children ever turned out finer. I've a host of sunlit memories of their childhood. My daughter's been married five years now. She visits me every week.

"My son's an artist. He travels the world. This summer he gave me a wonderful holiday in America. I'm now a widow, living alone. I live for my son's weekly letters and my daughter's visits. Every night I give thanks for the gift of these children."

Things could have gone wrong for this kind-hearted lady, but things wouldn't have turned out the way they did if she hadn't looked on the bright side . . .

BE thankful for the little things;
If you can talk awhile
With someone whom you love to see,
Just bringing you a smile.
If you can linger in the sun
To greet a bird that sings,
And gather daffodils again —
Be glad of little things.

THE FRIENDSHIP BOOK

G IVE me a sense of humour, Lord;
    Give me the power to see a joke:
To get some happiness from life
    And pass it on to other folk.

These four lines are known throughout the English-speaking world, and they sum up, in a neat and happy way, much of the duty of a Christian.

After all, however serious we are about our faith we need a touch of humanity as well as a touch of things spiritual ; and after looking to our own soul we need to help other pilgrims on the rough road of life.

D O you sometimes feel that no one does anything for nothing any more ?

To prove it's not true, let me tell you what happened to some friends of mine. On a little by-way near Invergowrie, Ann Nicol of Dundee spotted an old man sitting on a kitchen chair by the road-side, his cap pulled over his eyes for shade. Behind him, a piece of ground was carpeted thick with daffodils. Lying beside his chair were some big bunches of daffies. Ann called on her husband, Keith, to stop the car, then popped over.

" How much for a bunch? " she asked. The old smiled as he handed one over. " I dinnae charge, lass," he said. " If folk are keen enough to get out of their cars I ken they'll be appreciated. I've plenty growing here. It's the sun and the rain that brings them on. I just enjoy them."

I don't know the old man's name, or why he gives his daffies away so generously. But I can tell you his blooms brightened the day for the Nicols.

And for me, too !

SATURDAY—APRIL 19.

DID you hear about the Edinburgh grandfather who, when asked how he was, replied sadly, " Not so good, not so good. Only a few months ago I could walk round George Square, and enjoy it, but nowadays I can only manage halfway and back again !"

Which reminds me of the post office clerk who asked an old-age pensioner if she had any means of proving that the pension book she had presented really was hers.

" Look," said she with becoming dignity, showing him a photograph of herself, " doesn't this prove it ?"

And the post office clerk obligingly said it did !

These tales remind me of Aunt Annie, who remarked as her nephew sat down to tea, " Edmund, I don't think you washed your hands before tea, did you ?"

" No, Auntie," replied honest Edmund. " I didn't, but when I saw we were having brown bread I didn't think it mattered."

SUNDAY—APRIL 20.

HE which soweth sparingly shall reap also sparingly; and he which soweth bountifully shall reap also bountifully.

MONDAY—APRIL 21.

*D**OWN** in the dumps? Then consider*
  There's sunshine to follow the rain.
And after defeat, if you keep on your feet,
  There's some little triumph again.
Remember, when ready to sigh,
There's always a star in the sky!

TUESDAY—APRIL 22.

JAMES MACREA was born about 1677 of poor parents in or very close to Ayr. His father died young and his mother made a bare living as a washerwoman. Jim had no education apart from the little schooling he received from a local musician Hew McQuyre. Around 1692, Jim went to sea.

It was forty years before anybody in Scotland heard of him again. First with the East India Company, and later as Governor of Madras, he instituted such excellent reforms and so successfully abolished abuses and improved the fiscal administration that he was regarded as a genius. He returned to his native land in 1731, an enormously wealthy man.

It was what he did next that makes me like to remember the man. Finding he was without a relative in the world, he diligently sought out the family of his old teacher, Hew McQuyre, and adopted his five grandchildren, educating the young and endowing all.

Little could Hew McQuyre have known how the effects of his kindnesses would be multiplied and enlarged to benefit a future generation.

WEDNESDAY—APRIL 23.

SMILE if you like—but think about it, too!

Last week I heard the story of a Jew and a Christian who were arguing about their respective faiths.

Said the Jew, " Your whole religion is based on ours, anyway. Why, you even took the Ten Commandments from us."

" We may have taken them," retorted the Christian, " but you certainly can't say we've kept them !"

WHERE NOW?

Shall we take this road, shall we take that?
There's fun and adventure wherever we choose.
One way is hilly, another is flat,
The valleys for streams and the uplands for views.
So much to be seen, so much to be learned,
Till happily homeward our faces are turned.

DAVID HOPE

CRAFTSMAN'S HANDS

Simple tools are all you need,
But the hand and eye to guide them
Boast a more exclusive breed —
Not so easy to provide them.

DAVID HOPE

THE FRIENDSHIP BOOK

A TEACHER in an infants' class has passed on a little fellow's bit of philosophy. Some of us who are older might ponder it.

In a conversation about the weather, the youngster came up with this remark : " Please, Miss, clouds are to make you glad when the sun shines."

Perhaps you and I forget this truth. There could be no light if there were no darkness. We should never rejoice in good health if we never suffered pain or illness. If nobody ever lost a game, what fun would there be in winning ?

Thank God for the sunshine — but don't forget the clouds . . .

MY friend was recalling his boyhood days, and in particular the day when he was told to break up some coal in the cellar. Among others was one very large lump. The schoolboy handled a heavy hammer and struck tremendous blows with just no results whatever. He was a strong young laddie of a determined nature. That lump wasn't going to beat *him* ! So he set to work afresh, and struck one blow after another, all to no avail.

Then his father came down the steps and took in the situation with a glance. He grinned and turned the heavy lump of coal on its side. " Try again," he advised. My friend hit the offending lump again, and it split into a thousand fragments

Well, what couldn't be done one way was easily accomplished in another — a kind of parable of life. It's fine to be determined and persistent, but sometimes different tactics, a new approach, a gentler touch or a little more patience may do the trick.

SATURDAY—APRIL 26.

DR J. KILLOCH ANDERSON, medical superintendent of Glasgow Royal Infirmary, found in his mail a plain white envelope. Inside were four £5 notes and this message : " Please accept this donation as a gift on my retirement, which I'm very lucky and thankful to have reached, and with thanks for kindnesses in hospital. Yours sincerely, Anon."

Well, Dr Anderson was so thrilled he asked us to pass on his thanks. Now, and what d'you think ? One day soon after a letter reached me, in the same kind of envelope, with four £5 notes and this message : " Please put this to one of your good causes. Just a gift on my retirement, and to be thankful that I've reached the age. Yours sincerely, Anon."

Yes, it's grand to get a gift on your retirement, but isn't it even better to be grateful enough to make a gift, thankful for all the years you have had a job and the strength to do it, for the friends you've made and the satisfaction of a life well-spent.

SUNDAY—APRIL 27.

BLESSED be God . . . who comforteth us in all our tribulation, that we may be able to comfort them which are in any trouble.

MONDAY—APRIL 28.

E NDOW me, Lord, with strength to face
Life's biggest griefs and ills;
And give me, also, grace to bear
Life's little cares and chills.
Oh, make me patient, loving, kind —
And grant me, Lord, a quiet mind.

TUESDAY—APRIL 29.

NOT very long ago a rather shabby man walked into a car dealer's showroom in a Norwegian port, and inquired if they had sixteen new cars, all the same model.

After looking the customer up and down, the proprietor snapped, "Take your funny ways elsewhere."

The customer did. He crossed the road to another garage, and in a surprisingly short time he bought sixteen cars and paid for them in cash.

Explanation : the crew of a Norwegian fishing vessel had been enjoying an exceptionally good season, and on their last voyage had been discussing a suggestion that all sixteen of them should buy cars, making a single order and paying cash in order to get the greatest possible discount.

So the proprietor of one garage netted a very welcome order, and the other missed the biggest piece of business of the year !

Perhaps it is unfair to condemn the unfortunate garage proprietor, but it does show how appearances can be deceptive and that hasty judgments are dangerous.

WEDNESDAY—APRIL 30.

YES, she is a really gracious lady with an understanding heart. The Queen Mother, I mean.

In Leeds to confer the freedom of the city on the "Ark Royal," she spoke to a leading seaman lined up for review.

He couldn't answer. He had a cold and had lost his voice.

So the Queen Mum delved into her handbag and found him a lozenge !

The homely touch that endears her to us all.

MAY

THURSDAY—MAY 1.

MANY youngsters, especially boys, are not too keen on going to Sunday school!

Maybe some mothers will smile at this story from Roy Sutherland, of Newbattle, Edinburgh.

The Sunday school teacher was explaining a psalm to a class of small boys. " Now why," he asked, " do you think it's better to be a doorkeeper in the House of the Lord . . . ?"

For a moment there was silence. Then one wee lad piped up, " Because you'd be first out!"

FRIDAY—MAY 2.

A FEW years ago an Irish lass with laughing eyes left her home in Armagh to complete her nursing training in Western General Hospital, Edinburgh. Her name? Sheila Leonard, soon one of the best-loved nurses in the hospital.

Every patient became her friend. When they went home, she spent countless days off visiting the sick, the lonely and the old. They'll tell you Sheila's visits did more good than any medicine.

Then, at 24, Sheila became a district nurse in Sighthill, the calling she had set her heart on. Alas, it was to be tragically short. For Sheila was killed in a car crash.

But the story did not end there. For Sheila's young sister, Marian, decided to come to Edinburgh. She, too, would train as a nurse and try to follow the path that Sheila walked. One day, who knows, the badge her sister wore so proudly may be pinned on to her uniform.

Could Sheila have a finer tribute?

THE FRIENDSHIP BOOK

A SCHOOLTEACHER tells me a boy of seven wrote, " Wasps have stings so's you keep away from them."

I wish parents and teachers looked at life with the clear eyes of this small philosopher, and that all children were warned from time to time that bad things are things to keep away from.

The truth is no society can possibly afford not to inculcate in the young a knowledge of right and wrong, and to delight in the one and shun the other. This is the very basis of a sound society.

I know only too well this is not a popular idea at the moment ; but the fact remains that if children grow up with an awareness that dishonesty leads to trouble, and honesty is part of the routine of right living, our law courts will have less business, and there will be less hooliganism and fewer prison sentences. It is all too obvious to need stressing.

The Bible does not mention wasps, but it does say, very bluntly, that " the wages of sin is death." It's as true today as ever.

Bad things are things to keep away from.

SUNDAY—MAY 4.

CAST thy bread upon the waters : for thou shalt find it after many days.

MONDAY—MAY 5.

I WROTE a little letter —
It didn't take a minute.
I sent my love, and really
That's all that there was in it.
Back came a grateful word to say:
Thanks for your note — it made my day!

THE FRIENDSHIP BOOK

TUESDAY—MAY 6.

JENNY had worked ever since she was married.
When at last she gave up her job and stayed
at home I asked her what was the biggest change
in her life.

" Soup," she said. " You see, I make it myself now.
There's something about cutting up the vegetables,
and the colours, and the harvesty smell when you
put in the leeks and onions. And there's something
welcoming about it when Jack comes in for his
dinner . . ."

Nothing new about all this, of course; but it
was a grand discovery to make — and a fine com-
pensation for managing on less.

WEDNESDAY—MAY 7.

THE chigger is a mite which causes intolerable
itching if it once gets under your skin, so
much so that an American poet, who seems to
have suffered severely during harvest time, wrote
these lines :

Here's to the chigger, the bug that's no bigger
Than the end of a very small pin ;
But the itch that he raises simply amazes —
And that's where the rub comes in !

Well, this is just to remind us that little things
can cause infinite irritation. My Aunt Maggie was
the kindest and most placid soul I have ever known.
Occasionally she would invite a lonely old widower
to have a bowl of broth on a winter's day, but she
always contrived to busy herself elsewhere while
he spooned it, as he always made such a noise, it
was more than my aunt could endure.

The ability of the tiny chigger to irritate may well
remind us all to spare our relatives and friends from
having to endure our own little aggravating habits.

THE FRIENDSHIP BOOK

THURSDAY—MAY 8.

I KNOW someone who reads with her fingers and hears with her feet!

As you'll have guessed, Nan Love, of Lambhill, Glasgow, is blind. She reads with her fingers because she must use Braille, but how can she possibly hear with her feet? Well, Nan is also deaf. She can feel the vibrations of the floor as someone approaches. By sensing the difference in these vibrations, she can tell if the person coming towards her has a light or heavy step, whether they walk quickly or slowly, whether they tend to place one foot down more firmly than the other, and so on. Thus she has learned to recognise people by their footsteps, which she cannot even hear!

Our world is largely what we ourselves make of it. And I raise my hat to someone like Nan, whose courage has helped her to pierce not only her world of darkness, but of silence, too.

FRIDAY—MAY 9.

NO one knows who wrote these words, but they have certainly challenged many over the years:

Let me be a little kinder,
Let me be a little blinder
To the faults of those about me,
Let me praise a little more.
Let me be, when I am weary,
Just a little bit more cheery —
Let me serve a little better
Those that I am striving for.
Let me be a little meeker
With the brother who is weaker.
Let me think more of my neighbour
And a little less of me.

SATURDAY—MAY 10.

MISS Betty Taylor, a teacher, of Marchmont, Edinburgh, has kept a record of the sayings of children who have passed through her hands over the years.

One of her favourites is from the wee lad who hadn't been listening during a Bible story. " Robert," she said severely, " can you tell me how God knew that Adam and Eve had eaten the forbidden fruit ?"

Robert thought hard, and then he beamed.

" Please, miss," he cried, "it was because He saw the peelin's !"

SUNDAY—MAY 11.

BE not forgetful to entertain strangers : for thereby some have entertained angels unawares.

MONDAY—MAY 12.

A SPECIAL request from George Armes, of Ryan Place, Rotherham. George, a redoubtable pensioner with an independent spirit, feels that too many people these days want too much out of life. " Nobody's conscripted into a job nowadays," he declares. " Yet everybody who does a job of work seems to want the V.C. just for doing it !"

He feels that the following lines might put things in perspective. I don't know about that—but here they are :

To weep for what we cannot have
    Gets no one very far —
A pity to miss all the fun
    While searching for a star.
He's wise, who takes what each day brings,
And somehow makes the best of things.

THE BOND

The lady at our school today
Smiled and seemed to understand.
She spoke to me, I spoke to her,
I showed her how to paint your hand.

DAVID HOPE

D

HARVEST TIME

Late rays of Autumn sun
Cast patterns on the field,
Showing the work well done —
Another season's yield.

This is the basic toil
  Our lives depend upon.
Close-knit with sky and soil,
  The farmer's round goes on.

DAVID HOPE

SHARING

When first we planned our picnic
Days and days ago,
That we would have so many guests
We simply couldn't know.
It's just as well there's lots to eat,
So every swan can have a treat.

DAVID HOPE

THE FRIENDSHIP BOOK

A FRIEND of ours—a widow of 55—usually writes at least one letter a day.

When she lost her husband, and became a victim of arthritis, she was very unhappy. But gradually she came to realise how much letters could mean.

And she has learnt the truth of the lines :

Letters are a friend's best way
To brighten up another's day ;
And as I write I think of you —
It brightens up my own day, too !

IF you're like me you'll enjoy your Sunday visit to church all the better when some of your favourite hymns are included in the service. But, as my friend John Bunney, Consett, pointedly asks, do we really listen to what we sing ?

We sing " Onward Christian soldiers " — but have to be press-ganged into service.

We sing " Tell me the old, old story " — but are seldom there to hear it.

We sing " Take my silver and my gold " — but put our small change in the plate.

We sing " O for a thousand tongues " — but fail to use the one we have.

We sing " I need Thee every hour " — but grumble about spending one in church.

We sing " What a friend we have in Jesus " — but turn to Him only when we're in a jam.

We sing " I'm not ashamed to own my Lord " — but wouldn't dream of mentioning the fact outside the church.

We sing " Rise up, O men of God " — and lie in bed till twelve on Sunday mornings !

Honestly, now — do you really mean it . . . ?

THURSDAY—MAY 15.

MY friend, John Birkbeck of Stirling, sent me this story of Deveronside.

Cairnborrow Lodge, on the banks of the Deveron, was once the Scottish home of Sir Frederick Bridge, organist of Westminster Abbey.

He came up every summer, and brought many guests with him, one of whom was Sir John Stainer, organist of St Paul's Cathedral. So Sir Frederick approached Mr Guthrie, minister of the local kirk, and announced the presence of his distinguished guest. " I wonder," he said, " if you would be kind enough to allow Sir John to play the organ this Sunday instead of me?"

" Aye, surely," said the minister with a disarming smile. " We're not particular up here about who plays the organ!"

FRIDAY—MAY 16.

I REMEMBER a great-aunt of mine telling me about her grandfather.

" He was one of those men," she told me, " who was satisfied with nothing less than the best. A neighbour asked him to repair a door, and he searched for just the right bit of wood, and somehow cut it to fit perfectly ; and forty years later that house literally fell during a storm, and the only thing left standing was the door my grandfather had repaired."

I thought of this proud, careful craftsman not long ago when I heard of a farmer who was repairing a fence, and commented " Put in a bit of elm and forget it for twenty years—put in a bit of oak and forget it !"

Rather neat, I think ; a reminder that if a thing's worth doing, it's worth doing well.

SATURDAY—MAY 17.

THE day he was buried all the streets of Edinburgh were deserted except those leading to his grave.

Who was he?

He was a Scotsman who fought against one of the greatest enemies of mankind — pain!

Sir James Young Simpson pioneered the use of chloroform as an anæsthetic. He tested it on himself, and "came round like a drunken man," though his mighty brain became clear soon after.

It was not enough to discover anæsthetics. He had to spend his days defending their use—against ignorant medical men who said it was harmful, against those who contended it was immoral, and against religious men and women who declared he was interfering with the divine laws. But he fought on . . . and he won!

All the world owes a debt of gratitude to the man who wore himself out in serving humanity. As he was dying he asked how old he was, and a friend said, "Fifty-six."

"Oh, well," murmured the baker's son, "I just wish I'd been busier."

SUNDAY—MAY 18.

WHERE there is no vision, the people perish.

MONDAY—MAY 19.

WE need a lot of clever folk
To do big things today.
We need inspired leaders who
Can show us all the way . . .
And kindly folk who seem to be
Concerned about just you and me!

D

THE FRIENDSHIP BOOK

TUESDAY—MAY 20.

MRS MACMILLAN was always a worrier. But since entering an eventide home last autumn she has become years younger.

Soon after she had shed the daily chores and settled into a new routine in the Home, a pensioner in her late eighties gave her this piece of advice: "I've lots of aches and pains, my dear," she said, "and now my son has died, I do miss the little runs he used to give me in his car. *But I don't worry!* At my time of life there's little to worry about—and I advise you to go to bed when you are tired, get as comfortable as you can, and think about the pleasant things of life—you'll wake up feeling fine!"

That wise old body has passed on, but Mrs Macmillan has tasted her recipe for happiness, and finds it good. So she has asked me to pass it on to others, especially elderly folk!

WEDNESDAY—MAY 21.

ONE of the pleasantest tasks on holiday is the choosing of "mindings" to bring home; the gifts for the friends, the family, the neighbour who fed the cat or took in the budgie or watered the plants.

It takes a bit of time, it can cost a bit of money, but it's worth every penny. Ask the woman of the house, who usually does the choosing and buying. I think she'll say that it adds an extra day to the holiday, the day that she hands out the presents and hears everyone say, "Oh, you shouldn't have bothered!"

And if you're still not sure, watch her as the presents are unwrapped. You'll see that she looks as happy as the one who receives the gift.

THE FRIENDSHIP BOOK

PROFESSOR William Barclay is a well-known writer and broadcaster, and his appearances on television win wide audiences. How *did* he get through so much work in addition to his college lectures?

It was an overlap from his student days, he confesses, when he had to burn the midnight oil to study. He got up at two o'clock in the morning, worked till four, then back to bed till eight. His secret was that he worked while others slept.

One side of his life not generally known is that he is also an accomplished pianist and trained a choir of his divinity students in Trinity College, Glasgow. With them he gave concerts for charity to help struggling congregations.

It is the human touch of friendship which enhances his many talents.

YOU'LL have heard about the proposed Channel Tunnel, but have you heard of the cheerful Irish contractor who offered to dig it? Malone, by name, he ran a two-man firm—just himself and his son.

Of course, the politicians and financiers were sceptical. "Would you be able to handle it?" they asked. "Sure," smiled Malone. "Easy."

"How would you go about it?" he was asked. "Och," he went on, "I'd start diggin' at one side o' the Channel, and my son at the other, an' we'd meet in the middle."

"And what if you didn't meet?" pressed the chairman of the committee.

"Then, sorr," said Malone with a smile, "you'd get two tunnels for the price o' one!"

A touch of Malone's optimism would do us all good!

SATURDAY—MAY 24.

LAST century, a Scotsman, David Fife, sailed for Canada, and hired himself to a farmer.

But he missed Scotland so much that he returned, promising to send his master a Scots bonnet one day.

Well, David spotted just the bonnet his old boss might like in a Glasgow shop window. So he bought it and carried it under his arm while looking around the docks. A ship from Danzig was unloading wheat which, to David's practised eye, looked unusually fine. He helped himself to a handful, put it in the bonnet, and sent bonnet and grain to Canada.

Now the Canadian farmer sowed that wheat and reaped it many-fold. So he sowed again, and found that David's wheat thrived well, was hard, matured early—the perfect wheat for Canadian soil and climate. And in a few years that handful of grain produced such crops that all the granaries in Ontario couldn't hold it!

It was named Red Fife — and the millions of bushels of it grown in Canada all came out of a Scotsman's bonnet.

SUNDAY—MAY 25.

LET us not be desirous of vainglory, provoking one another, envying one another.

MONDAY—MAY 26.

THE folk who might complain but don't,
Who suffer loss, yet smile;
Who get more knocks than pence, but still
Will go the second mile —
These are the folk who, come what may,
Find much to sing about each day.

TUESDAY—MAY 27.

AS Mrs Duncan bathed and cuddled her new baby, she realised that Jeremy, aged four, was looking rather out of things.

"Do you think that Mummy doesn't love you now that you have a little sister?" she asked.

Jeremy nodded.

"Well," said his mother, "when baby's in bed, you and I will have a little talk. Just the two of us."

So, when the baby was asleep, Mrs Duncan explained that when a new baby comes the mother gets an *extra* supply of love for it, so that she doesn't have to take any away from her other children. Jeremy was much happier after that, and could watch his mother nurse the baby quite happily.

Sometimes a few moments of explanation can save hours of worry.

WEDNESDAY—MAY 28.

WHEN Mr and Mrs Henry Ford celebrated their golden wedding anniversary, a reporter asked Henry: "To what do you attribute your fifty years of successful married life?" Replied Henry Ford: "The formula is the one I've used in making cars—*Stick to one model!*"

THURSDAY—MAY 29.

IN one of her books, Jane Duncan, the much-loved Scottish novelist, has one of her characters being complimented on having a good memory.

"Yes, and I have got a lot of good things to remember," he replies.

I think you'll agree that's much more important. To have a good memory for bad things sours our lives.

THE Victorians have been called sanctimonious and over-religious. They are said to have been fond of stories like this one from the U.S.A.:

A small boy living in the downtown area of Boston joined a church Sunday school, and somebody who knew him said, " Say, now you've joined the Lord's people, why don't Christ send somebody to you with a pair of shoes ?"

The little fellow thought hard. Then, bursting into tears, he replied, " I guess the Lord do tell somebody to give me shoes . . . but I guess that somebody forgets !"

People often see others in need of help—financial help, a bit of comfort and compassion, an unexpected kindness—and, though they know they could do something, they just forget.

Somebody once said on a cold morning : " I was kept snug and warm last night by the blanket I gave away yesterday."

You understand ?

SATURDAY—MAY 31.

I LIKE the odd, sad little thought sighed by an old lady. " Age is funny. It is cherished in a tree. It makes cheese taste richer. It adds value to furniture and a bouquet to wine. Seems it is good for everything except me !"

But that tired body was the exception to the rule. At any rate, so it seems to me because I know men and women turned 80 who are bright and vivacious, busy and interested, with a kind of genius for enjoying every minute of every day, and putting far more into life than they can ever hope to get back . . . except, of course, the thrill of being very much alive.

MERRY MAY

> Children round the maypole dancing,
> Lightly skipping, gaily prancing,
> Back and forth and in and out,
> Weaving patterns round about,
> All the May Day girls and boys
> Welcome back the summer's joys.

E

DAVID HOPE

NATURE'S PALETTE

The dainty birch trees grouped around
Display their silvery sheen,
A challenge to the painter's skill
To capture such a scene.
But failure need not cause dismay —
It brings success some other day.

DAVID HOPE

JUNE

<u>SUNDAY—JUNE 1.</u>

A FAITHFUL friend is the medicine of life.

<u>MONDAY—JUNE 2.</u>

ON her thirteenth birthday Joan Nunn was given a beautiful Bible by her mother, white with a zipp round the edge. She didn't appreciate what it might mean to her one day, so, when a school friend offered her sixpence for it, she accepted it cheerfully.

As the years slipped by, Mrs Nunn often wished she'd never parted with it. On her wedding day she'd have given anything to have carried it as a bride. And when her mother died in 1965 the lost Bible came to mean more than ever to her.

Then, one day, Mrs Nunn was on a bus in Middlesbrough, ten miles from her home in Hutton Rudby. The conductress smiled at her and said, " Remember me?" Mrs Nunn confessed she didn't. " Well," the conductress reminded her, " we were at school together. You sold me a Bible for sixpence." Of course, Mrs Nunn remembered. She explained how she'd wished so often she'd kept the Bible, and told the conductress of her mother's death.

Two days later a parcel was delivered to Mrs Nunn's home. In it was the white Bible, and inside the cover her mother's familiar writing, " To Joan, with love from Mam."

That same morning Mrs Nunn wrote to thank the conductress. In the envelope she popped a sixpenny piece. She later sent a bouquet of flowers, but I'm sure the conductress will count that silver sixpence among her treasures.

TUESDAY—JUNE 3.

I UNDERSTAND this story was told by a nurse in a geriatric ward. A patient there—a tired and suffering old body—was required to supply some information, and to sign her name on a form. To the doctor who was helping her, she confessed hesitantly that she had never learned to write, and inquired if everything would be all right if she made a cross.

The doctor assured her that it would; and with a touch of inspiration and a wealth of understanding added, " You're in good company, my dear. Isn't that the way Jesus signed his name?"

WEDNESDAY—JUNE 4.

ALONE, I sometimes pause and say,
" You're in my loving thoughts today."
It seems there's no one there, and yet
I speak to those I can't forget;
Lest, being gone, they do not know
I think of them, and want them so!

THURSDAY—JUNE 5.

IN these trying days the Lady of the House and I often recall the old lady whose serenity was an inspiration to her neighbours when she gave the secret, " I thatched my house in the calm and now I'm not afraid of the storm."

William Blake, writer of the famous hymn, " Jerusalem," was once visited by an artist who complained he had lost all inspiration. Blake turned to his wife, " Why, Catherine, sometimes we lose the inspiration too. What do we do then?"

" William," she replied simply, " we kneel down and pray."

THE FRIENDSHIP BOOK

ONE day last century Captain Pendleton, of the British ship " Lord Gough," sighted the American vessel " Cleopatra " flying her flag at half-mast. The captain sent out a rescue party in high seas and facing a bitterly cold blizzard. Before the boat reached the doomed ship, the " Cleopatra " hauled down her flag. In sailors' language, she spelt out the message, " All is over. Leave us to our fate."

But the men of the " Lord Gough " rowed on, finding the crew still clinging to their sinking ship. Because of fine seamanship, great courage and a lot of luck, the boat returned safely with the rescued men; and eventually Captain Pendleton asked the captain of the " Cleopatra " why they had hauled down their colours.

" We signalled, ' Leave us to our fate,' " said the American captain, " because in such a storm we thought it wrong to tempt another crew to risk their lives in what was apparently a hopeless attempt."

Only as long as such a selfless and heroic spirit lasts can any country be said to be truly great.

NOW, here's to the mum who must cook,
    And wash up the pans and the pots.
A mum who can cope with the chores
    Or patiently care for the tots.
She scrubs or she mends till she aches;
    She bakes or she visits the store;
She never has time for a sit . . .
    She's helping her neighbour next door!
But don't be TOO sorry for Mum—
    She just hasn't time to feel glum.

SUNDAY—JUNE 8.

FOR it is written, As I live, saith the Lord, every knee shall bow to me, and every tongue shall confess to God.

MONDAY—JUNE 9.

ARE you tired out, a nervous wreck, feeling in desperate need of a rest?

Bishop Robert Gooden, a retired suffragan bishop of Los Angeles, does his own housework, prepares his own breakfast and sees to all the chores which fall to a man who lives alone. In one year he had some share in 55 Sunday services, 18 week-day services, four concerts in which he took part, six board meetings, 16 miscellaneous appointments. He found time for a flying visit to London where he attended services in Westminster Abbey, All Souls and St Paul's Cathedral, and interviewed a host of people. During the year he addressed a congregation of 1000 at a special High School service where he confirmed 80 pupils.

Some folk think ministers of religion have an easy task. Well, Bishop Robert Gooden has a pretty busy time of it—especially for a man coming up to 100.

So if you are feeling just about killed with work, enter the ministry if you dare.

TUESDAY—JUNE 10.

SUCCESS, of course, is very fine,
Yet sometimes giving in
Can save no end of trouble, and
Gain much more than a win.
To lose a heated argument
May prove the time was wisely spent!

THE FRIENDSHIP BOOK

I WAS thinking the other day of three people now in their forties. They were all born in Sheffield in 1929. All were patients of Dr C. G. Paine, and each in infancy was threatened with an eye trouble which could probably mean blindness, unless . . .

Dr Paine, once an assistant of Alexander Fleming, heard about a new discovery his old professor had made, and decided to ask him about it.

Fleming had the eye-drops made up. The babies' eyes were treated, and next day Dr Paine was astonished to see no trace of the trouble remained. The infection that had threatened to blind the little ones was gone.

That new drug, of course, was penicillin, and these three forgotten babies were the first people to be treated with it. Strangely, no one seemed to realise its possibilities. Ten years passed before a team of scientists stumbled on it and found new ways of using it. It was 1941 before it was hailed as a miracle drug.

Yet somewhere there are three people who can see because of it, and may never know how much they owe to the man who gave back life to millions the world over.

THE Lady of the House was having tea with Jennie recently.

She noticed Jennie, a widowed pensioner nearing 80, spread a piece of bread with both butter and jam. And Jennie noticed she'd noticed!

"Yes," she smiled, "I was brought up in the old-fashioned, thrifty way—butter *or* jam, but never both together. But I tell myself I'm still as thrifty. After all, I make the same piece of bread do for both!"

FRIDAY—JUNE 13.

IN the children's ward one Sunday afternoon a visitor distributed illustrated texts. One boy received a picture inscribed, " Your Best Friend is Jesus."

He looked at it doubtfully, and the nurse in charge saw him go into his locker, produce a note-book and a pencil and go round the beds asking each child a question, the answer to which he noted in his book.

Coming to the nurse, he reported, after con-sulting the results of his query, " I make it four votes for Jesus and six for Sister."

SATURDAY—JUNE 14.

I'VE heard of ships named after duchesses, streets after councillors and roses after gardeners. But never have I heard of a teapot named after a grannie.

Not until lately, that is, when a friend in Black-pool told me about Mrs Bessie Hudson, of Hands-worth Road. Mrs Hudson is a dab hand at making tea. Over the past 50 years she has brewed countless cuppas for all the guild nights, sales of work and other functions at her church.

Recently some of the St Paul's teapots needed replacing, and when the question of new ones was discussed, someone came up with a bright idea. A special chrome 30-cupper was ordered and secretly inscribed " Our Bessie." At a surprise ceremony the vicar launched it with a short speech and a packet of tea tied to the handle. Bessie acknowledged it with a regal curtsey and a light-hearted reply. A little piece of heart-warming nonsense, of course, though behind it lay a lot of esteem.

How much we all owe to the ladies whose tea-pots keep the social wheels merrily turning!

THE FRIENDSHIP BOOK

SUNDAY—JUNE 15.

THOUGH I be absent from you in the flesh yet am I with you in the spirit, joying and beholding your order, and the steadfastness of your faith in Christ.

MONDAY—JUNE 16.

FROM Mrs Marie Spear of Minehead in Somerset comes this quaint episode at the corner of a busy street. Mrs Spear used crutches then. She was standing near the pavement edge, watching the traffic surging by, when a car suddenly pulled up close by and a smiling lady—talking all the time—took her arm, and with a wave of her hand held up the traffic while the two of them hurried as fast as possible across the road.

Marie's mind was in a whirl, but the Good Samaritan beamed on her and talked so fast that the cripple couldn't get a word in edgeways. "There now, dear, you'll be all right, won't you?" said the helpful lady before darting back across the road and driving off, waving as she did so.

All a proof that this *is* a kind world after all!

But Marie couldn't help chuckling after she eventually recrossed the road at a convenient spot, and was picked up a moment later by her husband for whom she had been waiting as agreed!

TUESDAY—JUNE 17.

IT isn't sudden tragedy
Which breaks the shaken soul.
But cruel, irksome, bitter years
That take relentless toll
Of courage, strength and hope, unless
We have the grace of thankfulness.

WEDNESDAY—JUNE 18.

THINGS are not always as simple as they look.

Lloyd George confessed that if he was asked to speak an hour he needed little preparation, if half an hour at least six hours of thought, and if ten minutes he required a day's notice.

Martin Luther was once asked if he spoke to the doctors of divinity in his audience. " No," he replied, " to the washerwoman in the back pew."

And John Wesley read over his sermon to the servant lass of the household in which he happened to be staying and eliminated anything she could not understand.

Ladies will know that the simplest looking dress may be the most costly, and the menfolk realise often the wisdom in the simplicity of a little child.

THURSDAY—JUNE 19.

I CAME across a story a few days ago about the " Titanic," the liner declared unsinkable but which went down in mid-Atlantic on her maiden voyage, with over 1500 people drowned.

What caught my attention was that Captain Smith remained at his post without making the least attempt to save his life. He did desert it for a few minutes, however. That was to plunge into the water to save a drowning child.

With that little one he swam to one of the lifeboats and handed over his burden. Then he turned, swam back to the sinking vessel, and was seen standing calmly on the bridge as the ship vanished.

What is it buried in some of us which enables us to do our duty, or make the supreme sacrifice, or happily die in a great cause?

For so many, life is a poor thing. For some it is magnificent.

FRIDAY—JUNE 20.

LIZ HOGBEN, of Liverpool, had been reading about the difficulties widows often face and was moved to send me these thoughts :

No one whom they can turn to when they feel they cannot cope ;
No friendly voice to say to them, " You mustn't give up hope."
No happy smile to greet them when they're sad and tired and cold ;
No voices saying, " Glad you're home !" No caring hand to hold.
No one for them to talk to when they need a friendly ear,
No shoulder they can lean on when their hearts are full of fear.
No voice to say, " I love you," in the stillness of the night,
Just empty days in empty homes without an end in sight.
So when you're feeling weary, and your family gets you down,
Just spare a thought for all the lonely people in your town.
And try to smile at all the folk you meet along the way,
For a single little smile may brighten someone's lonely day.

SATURDAY—JUNE 21.

YOU'VE got a job that must be done?
A hard or tiresome chore?
Don't try to put it off, my friend,
But face it, I implore.
Thus will the task you'd feared to do
Become a victory for you!

SUNDAY—JUNE 22.

I SHALL light a candle of understanding in thine heart, which shall not be put out.

MONDAY—JUNE 23.

I KNOW I will not be popular with keen gardeners. But I have to confess I like daisies. I know all the arguments against them; and I readily concede that an abundance of daisies can ruin a lawn. Even the Lady of the House, gentle as she is, admits that.

But daisies by the roadside, in a field, by a brook, under trees in an orchard, ah, that is a different matter. I do not recall ever seeing the common daisy in a flower shop or a garden centre, and perhaps daisies cannot compare with carnations. Orchids are for duchesses—who would dare to present a daisy to a titled lady?

But not long ago I visited a patient in hospital. On his locker was an eggcup with a dozen daisies in it. The sick man pointed out the tiny bouquet and whispered, " Susie brought them yesterday; gathered them on waste land by the quarry. She's just four. They're very friendly little flowers, eh?"

I agreed. And I hope I shall never become so superior that I cannot welcome daisies . . . the flower which children with no money can give to folk they love.

TUESDAY—JUNE 24.

I WATCHED *her in the super store,*
  So small and old and grey.
Her eyes lit up—tomato soup
  With tuppence off today!
A tiny triumph—yet it still
Can give a housewife such a thrill!

WEDNESDAY—JUNE 25.

MARY DONNACHIE runs a pub. She also writes poetry — sincere little verses with a message for those who can read between the lines; and any money she makes from her poems she gives to those less fortunate than herself.

She is always thinking of others. She calls her customers " my dears," and warns them of the traffic when they leave. On Burns night she joins her regulars in a Burns Supper, a cosy family affair, and once, when she was ill, they ran her business between them till she was on her feet again.

Miss Donnachie, a modest person, sees nothing very special about this, but recently the town council decided to make her a freeman for "her unfailing kindness to everyone." And of all those who received their awards that night, none was applauded more loudly and generously than Mary.

A small award, perhaps, but very well deserved.

THURSDAY—JUNE 26.

DURING a shower not very long ago the Lady of the House popped in to see one of her old dears.

Maggie, who lives alone and is turned 80, was concerned about her. She insisted my wife remove her damp coat and hang it over a chairback before the fire. And she wouldn't stop fussing till the kettle boiled and each of them sipped a cup of tea.

It isn't surprising that once the two were settled down they discussed the weather, Maggie remarking in her bright, birdlike way, " There's an old saying, dear, that it never rains but what it pours. I don't hold with that. I've had a lot of trouble in my day but I still say—*It never rains but what it stops!*"

Maggie's version is the one I prefer — don't you?

E

FRIDAY—JUNE 27.

KING EDWARD VII had been lunching in Hove with his friend, David Sassoon, and as he came out he was approached by a schoolboy who asked the time. The King consulted his watch. " Half-past three," he said.

" Half-past three?" the schoolboy repeated. " Crumbs, it's later than I thought. They say the blooming old King's inside this house, and I've been hanging around since one o'clock! If it's *that* time I ain't waiting no longer . . . he ain't worth it !"

King Edward, turned sixty, never quite grew up. Instead of being annoyed, he was tickled pink by the loyal but weary laddie. " You're right," he declared warmly. " Absolutely right, sonny. He just ain't worth it. Anyhow, there's no need for you to wait any longer. I'm the blooming old King, and here's something to remember me by."

One or two coins changed hands, and the astonished laddie went off with his head in a happy whirl.

SATURDAY—JUNE 28.

WE do not always say what we mean. Here's the story of the stolid Yorkshireman who was a witness in a court case. " Tell me, my good man," said counsel, " are you acquainted with any of the jury?"

" Aye," was the prompt answer. " Ah reckon Ah know more than half of 'em."

" Would you be willing to swear you know more than half of them?" counsel demanded.

" If it comes to that," declared the forthright Yorkshireman, " Ah'm willing to swear Ah know more than all of 'em put together !"

THE FRIENDSHIP BOOK

A READER sent me this notice she found in a
church in Grasmere, Westmorland:
> If, after church, you wait a while,
> Someone may greet you with a smile.
> But, if you quickly rise and flee,
> We'll all seem cold and stiff, maybe.
> The one beside you in the pew
> Is perhaps a stranger too.
> All here, like you, have fears and cares:
> All of us need each other's prayers.
> In fellowship we bid you meet,
> With us, around God's Mercy Seat.

HAVE you heard the story of a traveller in the
East who, while journeying by train, picked
up a small book and began reading it? Suddenly he
realised that the book was part of the Christians'
Bible, and, greatly incensed, he tore it into shreds
and threw the bits and pieces out of the window
to be scattered by the wind.

That man imagined he was stopping the gospel
message reaching others. It never occurred to him
that he was actually spreading abroad the good news.
For it happened that a plate-layer picked up one of
the scraps of St John's Gospel, and read the words,
" Bread of Life." He told himself that was what he
needed, and kept asking where he could get it, till
somebody gave him a copy of the complete gospel
—and reading it, the coolie came to believe in Christ
and His gift of abundant life, and though ignorant,
he gathered others about him, sharing his faith
with them.

Whatever you may think of the Bible, it takes a
lot of destroying!

JULY

TUESDAY—JULY 1.

THIS reads like a fairy story come true.

Once, in the province of Grasse, in France, there lived a beautiful young girl who fell in love with a young farmer, Pierre. Her father, however, vowed to marry her to a rich suitor.

" I will never let Pierre marry you unless he can bring to me 20,000 crowns," he declared in contempt. Now Pierre was not a very successful farmer, but he could grow beautiful roses.

" If only I could turn those roses into money," sighed the love-sick Pierre.

Soon afterwards his neighbours were astonished when he began rooting up his vines and trees and planting in their place roses and violets. Pierre crushed the flowers, and from them made the scent which made him rich, and for which the province has become famous.

So the perfume within your price today was perhaps made possible by the vision of a youth in love.

WEDNESDAY—JULY 2.

*N*OW *some folk say that shopping is*
*   The worst of all the chores;*
But I LIKE shopping round because
*   It takes me out of doors.*
I see what is a-going on—
*   Are prices up or down?*
It's fun in stores to chat with folk
*   Like lively Mrs Brown!*
And if I nab a bargain—say,
*   I feel life's going just my way!*

THURSDAY—JULY 3.

SOME years ago, a boy arrived in a town in America and going up to his room in the evening, he started to read his Bible. A fellow room-mate who saw him confessed, " I read my Bible, too." So they read together.

Next morning as they were leaving one said to the other, " Wouldn't it be a good idea if others were able to share the Bible as we have done." So they left their Bibles for others to read.

The idea caught on. A society was founded to place Bibles in hotels. They called themselves the Gideonites, from the Bible story of the few chosen from the many to fight with Gideon.

It spread to other lands and not only to hotels, but to prisons, hospitals and schools—in fact, anywhere where folk might be looking " for something to read." From a small beginning in friendship a world-wide movement had started.

FRIDAY—JULY 4.

TWO visitors from Australia were looking for postcards in a shop in Galashiels.

Now, I would have expected them to choose something striking ; a picture of a Border reiver, or a ruined castle, an old abbey, or a celebrated beauty spot.

But what do you think they wanted ? Something green. You see, they were so taken with our green grass and trees, our leafy roads and grassy verges that they had to let the people at home see for themselves how beautiful these things were.

Of course, it is the rain that makes the soft greenness that they enjoyed ; and they loved that, too.

Don't we take our blessings for granted ?

SATURDAY—JULY 5.

ROBERT HALL became a famous preacher, though, as a boy, he must have felt it was beyond his wildest dreams. A cripple, he could not walk to school. A friend carried him there on his back each day.

He learned so well that he attained entrance to Aberdeen University, and, while there, a surgeon noticed him and decided he could help him to walk by an operation. So Robert Hall achieved his dream of being a minister.

A story of triumphant courage. But it would not have been possible without the help that others gave : the school dominie, the professors and the skilled surgeon.

But most of all the schoolboy who began it all by carrying Robert Hall on his back to school.

SUNDAY—JULY 6.

LET no man seek his own, but each his neighbour's good.

MONDAY—JULY 7.

DURING the last war, Mrs Violet Howlett, a London housewife, was injured in an air raid, and rushed to a hospital which the Queen Mother was visiting.

Violet was unconscious when the Queen Mother passed through the ward. Missing her has always been one of the biggest disappointments of her life.

So, recently, friends wrote to Clarence House, telling her of Violet. Back from the Queen Mother came a letter inviting Violet to tea.

If you have ever wondered why the Queen Mother is so well loved, there is the answer.

EASTER BONNETS

Our bonnets welcome Easter —
We know they're smart, it's true.
But what's beneath the bonnets
Is worth inspection, too.

DAVID HOPE

SETTING OFF

A long, hard tramp on a perfect day,
What could be better fun?
The miles fly past when the heart is gay
And the world laughs in the sun.

DAVID HOPE

TUESDAY—JULY 8.

HAS it ever occurred to you that prayers have been said on the moon?

It strikes me as amazing and challenging, and I came upon this miracle of our time when reading about Colonel James Irwin, one of the Apollo 15 astronauts. At one time he was a test pilot in the American Air Force. Things were going his way till he made a crash landing—and everyone knew then his flying days were over.

He knew it, too. As he lay in hospital he kept asking God why this misfortune had come to him. Why? But his rebellion gave place slowly to acceptance of his handicap, then, curiously, to a new faith in God's goodness. From that moment he made incredibly rapid progress to complete health. So much so, he was chosen to train as an astronaut. In the end he left this planet below, rose into space, and landed on the moon, where his footprints remain.

And while moving in the silence and loneliness of the moon he prayed.

Yes, prayer belongs not only to this tiny earth but to the whole wide world of space.

WEDNESDAY—JULY 9.

MY bit of garden's nothing much,
  But all the summer through
I keep it colourful and sweet,
  With flowers—just a few.
I seem to have green fingers—so
  I brighten up my plot.
I like the good old-fashioned blooms,
  And talk to them a lot.
And, best of all, most every day,
I've something nice to give away!

THE FRIENDSHIP BOOK

A VISITOR, passing a building site, was curious as to what the workmen were building. "What are you doing?" he asked one, to receive the terse reply, "I'm digging a hole," as if he could not see that for himself. The second replied briefly, "I'm mixing cement," and a third, "I'm building a wall."

But the fourth, with the light of interest in his eyes, declared, "We're building a cathedral. *I've seen the plan.*"

Robert Louis Stevenson, walking in Fife, came upon a man mucking out a byre and, to the writer's delight, their conversation ranged over almost every subject from politics and literature to religion.

It was then R.L.S. declared to the friend with him, "He that aye sees something beyond is never wearied."

A MAN was rejoicing in the spring as he whistled along. He encountered a lad who challenged him, "I can whistle better than that, mister," and thereupon burst into the song he had heard the blackbird whistle that morning. In reply, the man carolled the song of a thrush.

Entering into the competition, the boy retorted with the whistling of a canary, to which the man replied with the song of a lark ascending into the sky and fluttering with joyful wings.

The boy listened with wonder and realised that he could never beat that. Then he burst out, "Hey, mister, if you can whistle like that why did you whistle like yon?"

A good question to some of us who may be content with less than the best.

SATURDAY—JULY 12.

THERE are always at least two points of view. For example, you may regard today as just another day to be lived, much like yesterday and all the other days you have managed to get through in spite of troubles, cares, disappointments and difficulties.

But you can also look at today quite differently because, as somebody has said : Today is the first day of the rest of your life.

It's a refreshing point of view. It makes this ordinary day notable — the first day of all the years you are going to live, and therefore a chance to live it, and the ones that follow, a bit more finely.

Worth thinking about, isn't it?

SUNDAY—JULY 13.

HE loveth righteousness and judgment : the earth is full of the loving-kindness of the Lord.

MONDAY—JULY 14.

FORTY Glasgow grannies had been looking forward for weeks to a trip to the Trossachs and Loch Earn. At last came the long-awaited day after a spell of gloriously fine weather—and the dawn brought rain.

It never stopped raining all that day. The grannies could see nothing from the coach windows. When they arrived in Callander, they were met by a leaden sky, pools on pavements and half-flooded streets.

It was old Mrs Mackay who saved the day. " Oh, well," she said with a grin, " one thing's sure. Nobody's going to suffer from sunstroke !"

When things go wrong, we can still make the best of them !

TUESDAY—JULY 15.

THE visitor thought it was the most friendly church he had ever been in, for the little girl sitting beside him greeted him with, " Good morning." When the first item of praise was announced she handed him a hymn book and for the scripture lesson her own Bible.

Then when the text was given out she squeezed a peppermint into his hand.

Do you wonder that the visitor returned and ultimately joined that church ?

WEDNESDAY—JULY 16.

LORD, comfort all who have to lie
In bed on summer days.
Please grant them patience to endure
In secret, wondrous ways;
And give the folk who nurse and bless
A gentle touch — and kindliness.

THURSDAY—JULY 17.

THE housewife was grumbling about the price of vegetables. " Potatoes are ridiculous," she said. " They ought to be getting cheaper by now."

" That's right, they should," agreed the assistant.

" And lettuces ! They're not even tender——"

" They're not," said the assistant, smiling sympathetically.

" And look at apples. You can't buy them."

" No, it's terrible."

" You know," said the housewife, outside the shop, " I just couldn't get up a good argument with her."

Isn't there something about a soft answer . . . ?

FRIDAY—JULY 18.

I'D like to tell you about Bob Barclay.

Bob was a steelworker, one of the first Scots to go down to Corby and take a job in the foundries there. He never regretted it. Life was good. Then, in an accident, Bob lost both his legs.

Yet within a year Bob was back at work, walking on artificial legs. Enough of a triumph in itself, you'd imagine. But not for Bob. He decided he'd never be content until he'd proved he could do anything on his tin legs that he would have been able to do on his real ones.

His first challenge was to walk five miles. When he'd accomplished that, he looked for new targets. He climbed Blackpool Tower, and up the steep hill to Edinburgh Castle. Then he went to London, and climbed the 258 steps to the Whispering Gallery in St Paul's Cathedral. And though each was a triumph, it only made Bob look for greater tests to set himself, fresh Everests to conquer.

Maybe faith can or cannot move mountains. But as Bob has shown, it can certainly help you over them!

SATURDAY—JULY 19.

AT a church in Ontario, attended by friends of ours, there's a room where young mothers may leave their babies during the morning service. On the wall of that room is a text, from 1st Corinthians, chapter 15, verse 51.

Nobody knows who pinned it there, but few can resist a smile as they peep in at the line of babies in carrycots and prams, then see the text framed above them.

It reads : " We shall not all sleep, but we shall all be changed . . . !"

THE FRIENDSHIP BOOK

LET all bitterness, and wrath, and anger, and clamour, and evil speaking be put away from you, with all malice : and be ye kind one to another.

MONDAY—JULY 21.

I HEARD recently of an American professor of physics who was trying to teach the quantum theory to his students. He confessed to a friend : "When I explained it the third time I suddenly understood it myself."

And this admission contains a great truth. It is by teaching we learn. I remember years ago a very fine minister of religion telling me : "You'll be shocked, but I have to admit that all the time I was a student at college I could not believe in God as a father. I tried to. I read the required books. I listened to sermons and lectures, but the lurking doubt remained. But soon after I became an ordained minister I had to deal with a man in great trouble, and it was while trying to persuade him that God is, and that God cares, that in a flash I was convinced of the truth I was saying."

TUESDAY—JULY 22.

IF you make up your mind today
To look for pleasant things,
For smiles or sunshine, bits of fun,
Surprises fortune brings ;
If you are slow to find the worst
But quick to spot the best,
You won't be sorry for yourself
But count yourself well blessed.
It's up to you to make today
As sad as sad or bright and gay !

WEDNESDAY—JULY 23.

SYLVIA TAYLOR, of Newcastle, has been telling me about her old friend, Florrie.

Florrie, a faithful member of her church for 75 years, was recently visited by a couple of doorstep disciples—zealous young men, eyes aflame with passionate sincerity, eager to claim every soul for their own religious sect.

" Good-morning," said the taller of the two, with an earnest gaze at Florrie. " Have you found Jesus yet?"

Feigning alarm—but with a twinkle in her eyes— Florrie replied, " Mercy, son—I didn't even know He was lost !"

He who crosses swords of faith with Florrie does so at his peril !

THURSDAY—JULY 24.

I VISITED Mrs Carruthers the other day. It was some time since I had seen her, but she made me welcome, asked me in, and ushered me into an armchair. I said *she* must sit there. She said *I* must—and we laughed.

Then she confessed. " You *must* sit there," she told me. " I am stone deaf in the right ear, but I have one blessing—a good left ear. I'm too old to care if people know I am partially deaf... but when I was twenty years younger—about sixty, you know—I contrived one way or another to keep my deafness a secret."

" You certainly tricked me," I told her. " But I'm so sorry to learn you have this affliction."

" Oh," she assured me, " on the whole it is, I think, a blessing. When I was staying in London, traffic roared by all night. So I just turned on my left side in bed, and slept like a top !"

FRIDAY—JULY 25.

WHAT is wrong with the world?

Abraham Lincoln came near to the answer when one day he laid hands on a couple of small boys who were about to fight. They yelled as he led them home ; and a neighbour, hearing the fuss and seeing the gaunt man keeping tight hold of the youngsters, called out, " What's wrong?"

With a grin, Lincoln replied : " The same trouble as the world is in. One of these lads has a nut, and the other one wants it."

That's the trouble—in a nutshell !

SATURDAY—JULY 26.

SOME years ago Ella Stothart came to Dundee as a lass in her twenties to be a welfare officer for the blind. It was a job that would be a challenge to most people. To Ella, it must have been a far greater challenge, for she herself is blind. But I'm sure her sense of humour has helped her as much as anything. This story will show you what I mean.

She was taking a shortcut through a cul de sac she knew quite well. She found the step with her stick, tapped her way up the slope and was about to go through (as she thought) a gap in the wall, when a friendly voice hailed her.

" Hello," it said. " Are you part of this removal?" Yes, you've guessed—she'd walked right inside a furniture van that was parked at the end of the cul de sac !

No one enjoyed the joke more than Ella !

SUNDAY—JULY 27.

BLESSED are the merciful : for they shall obtain mercy.

SHOWING HOW

There's any amount of astonishing things
For folk to dig up on the beach
And young 'uns are never too little to learn
When old 'uns are willing to teach.

DAVID HOPE

F

EARLIEST MEMORIES

A croft close-set beneath a hill,
The murmur of a burn;
The exile's heart in distant lands
To these will fondly turn.

Though fortune bless his every step
And honours crown his way,
The house he'll see, the water hear,
Until his dying day.

DAVID HOPE

REVERIE

Sometimes we're never less alone
Than when alone we seem.
For oh! what store of golden days
Come flooding back in dream!
And what a host of friends await
When we let memory hold the gate!

DAVID HOPE

THE FRIENDSHIP BOOK

ONE November day, a rose bush was delivered to an address in Ayrshire, and John and Jean were delighted. A friend in England had sent the gift. John wrote to thank him, saying he would plant the bush next day.

But John passed away in his sleep that night. Six days later the broken-hearted Jean *made* herself plant that rose bush in a sunny corner of the little garden John had loved so much.

The following year Jean had no roses from the gifted bush—even now she does not know quite why, and all year she gave the matter scant attention. Losing John so suddenly—he was only 58—had been a terrible shock, and nobody seemed able to comfort her or bring a smile to her pale face.

But a miracle happened the very next summer. The weak, neglected, unpruned rose bush Jean had planted—as a kind of memorial to John—blossomed of its own accord. It displayed a profusion of glorious red blooms which have been like fire in that corner of the garden—and somehow Jean's heart has at last been comforted. She has been able to weep . . . and now she can smile again.

WE climbed into the motor coach,
The driver cracked a joke,
And off we went—a-singing songs,
Us forty friendly folk.
We left the noisy streets behind,
We passed fields full of gold;
We tasted Blackpool's good fresh air—
And ice-cream, smooth and cold.
And in the golden twilight we
Felt we had been in famed Capri!

WEDNESDAY—JULY 30.

KIRK beadles, as church officers are known in Scotland, were often characters whose sayings were cherished. I like the story of the one who was so cheerful that in any problem or to any complaint he had the inevitable answer, " It might have been worse."

One Sunday morning he found the minister in the vestry looking very sorry for himself and asked what the matter was. " Oh," lamented the minister, " last night I dreamed I was dead."

The usual comment came, " It might have been worse." " What!" retorted the cleric. " What could have been worse than that ?"

" Well," replied the beadle, " it might have been true."

THURSDAY—JULY 31.

G. K. CHESTERTON said, " God must love ordinary people best for He has made so many of them."

There have been generals who have made their name in history, but they have had to depend on the countless unnamed soldiers who fought the battles.

There have been heroines whose names are remembered, but countless more housewives whose only thought was to do their daily acts of self-sacrifice.

The few in the board-room but the many on the shop floor. The judge on the bench but the twelve ordinary men and women who serve as jury and decide the verdict. The parliamentarian but the ordinary citizen who has the power to elect.

So if you think you are just an ordinary person you are the most important of all.

AUGUST

ONE institution that makes an appeal to the generosity of most of us is Dr Barnardo's homes for orphans and homeless children.

This is how it all started. The doctor taught in a Sunday school for poor children in London. One day, after school, he noticed a boy clinging to the comfort of the hot pipe. "Why don't you go home?" he asked the boy. "Please, sir, I have no home to go to," was the reply. "What about your parents?" was the further question. "I got no father or mother," explained the boy.

"Where do you stay then?" asked Dr Barnardo, wondering. The boy led him to a nearby vault. "I stay in 'ere," he said, "with a lot of other boys." So impressed was Dr Barnardo with the need of those boys that he immediately began to devote all his energies to setting up a home for them.

The one home has grown to many all over Britain. To give is to share in this great work of love and friendship to the homeless child.

RECENTLY I heard of a wee boy, aged three and a bit, who met a neighbour one morning.

They chatted for a while. Then, to keep the conversation going, Mrs Mackay asked Robbie how old he was now.

"Two," he replied promptly.

Mrs Mackay smiled. "Oh, no, Robbie," she said. "I think you're older than that."

Without batting an eye, Robbie replied, "Yes— but I can't say fwee!"

F

THE FRIENDSHIP BOOK

SUNDAY—AUGUST 3.

THE ear of jealousy heareth all things.

MONDAY—AUGUST 4.

I AM told she was young and pretty. She boarded
a bus, sat down, opened her purse, coloured
and said to the conductor who was advancing for
her fare, " Oh, I'm sorry. I haven't a penny."

" Pity," was the laconic reply. " You'll just have
to get off at the next stop !"

For a moment the girl looked upset. Suddenly,
she smiled. " Oh, well," she said quite good-
naturedly, " the walk will do me good."

She said it with a smile, and instantly a woman
passenger piped up : " Sit down, my dear. You
can let me pay the fare !"

I am reminded of an American saying : A smile
is a curve that can set a lot of things straight.

TUESDAY—AUGUST 5.

IT is a great day in the children's ward when it
is visited by some celebrity.

It has its amusing moments too. One child,
clamouring for a share of the gifts the visitor had
brought, was asked by her, " Aren't you just a little
impatient?" " No," replied the child indignantly,
" I'm a little 'er patient "—for the gift depended on
the sex. A nurse remembers the visit of the Lord
Mayor, led round by the city officer, in gorgeous
uniform and complete with mace.

As the party left, one child began to cry and
shout, " Bring him back . . . bring him back !"
" Who?" asked Sister, " the Mayor?" " No,"
informed the child, " his slave." A good thing that
dignified official was out of earshot!

WEDNESDAY—AUGUST 6.

*I*F *someone wants a word with you,*
Be patient and stand still.
You never know how hard life is
For those grown old or ill.
To let them have their little say,
May give them comfort for the day.

THURSDAY—AUGUST 7.

I HEARD a curious confession the other day from a highly successful business man who has won fame and devoted himself to much charitable work. Speaking of his childhood, he told me this :

" When I was about nine I had an elder brother, Tom. I worshipped him. He was kind and thoughtful. He would do just anything for me—give me his pocket money (which wasn't much), or play ball with me or mend a broken toy. Then he became ill, and I chanced to overhear a conversation between my parents, and suddenly realised that Tom was very ill, indeed dying, of what we then called consumption.

" From that day my school work went to pieces, anxiety and fear made me curiously quiet—except when I was with Tom. Then I tried to be funny. I read to him. I made up adventures . . . anything, anything at all to make that pale, thin face light up with a smile. And at night I pulled the bedclothes over my head and sobbed myself to sleep. And still Tom lives in me."

A sad loss, you may say. But fate works in strange ways, and I sometimes wonder if the little brother would have become such a famous man if Tom had lived and the other had continued to have him to lean on.

FRIDAY—AUGUST 8.

JUST a thought for today:
A man needs a woman to take care of him so that she can make him strong enough for her to lean on.

SATURDAY—AUGUST 9.

MANY a father's proudest day is when his son decides to follow in his footsteps.

With five sons, I'm sure old Dr Coutts, minister of Milngavie, could have expected one of his boys to become a minister, too. But Dr Coutts knew a young man must make up his own mind and to each of them he said the same: "If you really want to be a minister, well and good. But don't do it just to please me. All I want is that, whatever you choose, you do your best."

None of the boys did become a minister. Robin, the eldest, born deaf, was a brilliant scholar, and went on to become an engineer. Walter is now Sir Walter Coutts, a former Governor-General of Uganda. Ben became Captain Ben Coutts, one of Scotland's best-known farming personalities and a broadcaster. Philip was Minister of Labour in Uganda, and now heads an important Government Board there.

Frank became a soldier. He rose to command the Army's Highland area, and retired as a brigadier.

How proudly those five boys have lived up to their father's challenge.

SUNDAY—AUGUST 10.

WHOSOEVER will lose his life for my sake, the same shall save it.

MONDAY—AUGUST 11.

I LIKE weddings, and, with the Lady of the House, have been present as guest at not a few. What expectancy is stirred as we wait for the bride, imagining her driving up to the church, being photographed, walking down the aisle on her father's arm and taking up her position beside her future husband. Many a girl has lived for the day and gone over in her mind every detail.

Waiting thus the other day, my thoughts wandered to the bridegroom—also waiting. He has to kick his heels in the vestry as the minutes slip so slowly past, wondering if the clock has stopped. Will she turn up in time or exercise the privilege of the bride to be a few minutes late?

Probably he is going over the service in his mind wondering if he is word-perfect. All he can do is wait. One bridegroom summed up his feelings when the minister asked, " Wilt thou take this woman to be thy wife?" and he answered, " I *wilt.*"

So while you are waiting for the bride on her big day, spare a thought for the bridegroom waiting for his big ordeal.

TUESDAY—AUGUST 12.

FROM Mrs Kathleen Fern, of Newport, comes a verse which sums up my feelings about finding fault in things and people.

Don't look for the flaws as you go through life.
And even when you find them,
It's wise and kind to be somewhat blind
And look for the virtue behind them.
For every cloud has a beam of light
Somewhere in the shadows hiding—
It is better by far to look for the star
Than the spots on the sun abiding .

WEDNESDAY—AUGUST 13.

THE Very Rev. Andrew Herron tells of a farmer in Houston who was expecting an expert to call and advise about some agricultural problem.

"And what is an expert?" asked Mr Herron.

"Oh, he's just an ordinary farmer 50 miles away from here," was the reply.

We can all talk big when we're far enough away from our neighbours.

THURSDAY—AUGUST 14.

SOME of an older generation may remember the Rev. John McNeill, in his day a popular Scottish preacher and evangelist, who attained a nationwide reputation for his eloquence and sense of humour. It was he who when called to be a minister in Edinburgh, coined the oft-quoted phrase of the Capital as being " East-windy and west-endy."

But he never lost his human touch. He had been a railway porter at one time in the West, and retained his blunt and homely manner in the pulpit.

One story he delighted to tell was of visiting a poor old woman in the High Street with the help he knew she very much needed. At repeated knocking he could find no one to answer. But meeting the woman in the street afterwards he told her of his visit. " Was it you?" she said, adding as her reason for not opening the door, " I thought it was the man for the rent." His eye gleamed with characteristic humour as he shouted, " Woman! You thought it was the man for the rent and all the time it was John McNeill *with* the rent."

Many a time after he told the story to illustrate the way of God's providence to those in need.

SKILL OF GENERATIONS

Long ere history began
Walls were built by early man
And there are among us still
Those who have the ancient skill,
Men with knowledge in their bones
Of the way to handle stones.

DAVID HOPE

G

PATIENCE

It's fine when we can challenge fate
And problems brush aside;
But comes a day when all must wait
In patience for the tide.

DAVID HOPE

FRIDAY—AUGUST 15.

*I*T'S *when you feel you can't keep on,*
You to yourself should say —
There is no care too big for prayer,
No load which day by day
With God I cannot wholly share,
No fear of which he's unaware.

SATURDAY—AUGUST 16.

NOT long ago Jean's husband went off to work —
and never came back alive.

Knowing how gentle and almost fragile Jean was, her friends could not imagine her carrying on with the household chores, caring for the two very small bairns and all the rest without John.

And it looked at first as if they were right. Right up to the funeral she continued to weep. She became ill. The doctor was worried. Some hours after the funeral, however, her sister opened the living-room door and said, almost timidly, " I've got the bairns in the bath, love, but they keep asking you to dry them and put them to bed." For a moment Jean stared uncomprehendingly. Then, suddenly, she jumped up, went upstairs, bathed the children, saw them into their pyjamas, tucked them up in bed and kissed them good-night. From that moment Jean took over again.

She realised that, although she had lost her beloved John, she still had her precious bairns— *his* bairns . . .

SUNDAY—AUGUST 17.

LET us therefore follow after the things which make for peace, and things wherewith one may edify another.

MONDAY—AUGUST 18.

THERE is a story told of Paganini, the amazing violinist, who, while playing before a celebrated audience, had the misfortune to break every string but one of his violin. Instead of throwing down his instrument as useless, he grinned at his audience and said, " Ah, now one string and Paganini !"

Then he played as never before—and won unprecedented applause.

That, I suggest, is the way to play the game of life.

TUESDAY—AUGUST 19.

THIS is a story of a schoolboy who had his right hand blown off when he was experimenting in a chemistry laboratory. As a result of the accident the boy suffered much pain and became sullen. He had been a merry lad, but after losing his hand he became rebellious, bitter and inclined to self-pity. His parents did all they could for him but could not get him to go out and meet people again.

One day his father said that a preacher visiting the neighbourhood wanted to see him. The boy said he didn't want the preacher in the house. " He's a jolly fellow," his father went on. " And daft about football."

In the end the laddie mumbled, " All right, I'll see him."

What a shock the schoolboy had when in came a big man with twinkling eyes and a hearty laugh, in spite of the fact that he had only one arm—and that was his left one. Despite the difference in their ages, the handicap each suffered from formed an immediate link. The man and boy became great friends, and that schoolboy is now a happy and useful member of society.

THE FRIENDSHIP BOOK

MISS MARY COWHIG, of Bootle, Lancashire, told me this tale about a violet.

One day last century a Russian princess found a violet, planted it in the middle of a lawn and asked her father, the Czar, to have it guarded.

Year after year a sentry stood there—summer and winter. One sentry following another till one day an Ambassador asked why there was a guard in the middle of the lawn.

It was an embarrassing moment because nobody knew—a sentry had always stood there, always . . . However, eventually a very old man told the story of the princess's violet, so the latest sentry was dismissed simply because there was no violet to protect . . . and a few days later up popped a modest violet on the very spot where generations of sentries had stood!

Miss Mary does not know if the tale is true or not—but it certainly shows how enduring some of the most delicate things can be.

MANY tales are told of Presidential tours in America. The one I like is about Theodore Roosevelt.

He was making a speech, after stepping out of a train, to a crowd on the platform. All the time he was speaking he noticed a little girl, poorly clad, watching him. The minute the speech was concluded, the President pushed through the crowd, shook hands with the little girl, and turned back to the train which was already moving. It only took a moment, but it was an incident that she would remember and cherish all her life. The truly great are the truly considerate.

FRIDAY—AUGUST 22.

WATCHING a loved one suffer can be worse than enduring pain yourself.

There comes to mind a woman whose sister was discharged from hospital as incurable. For over two years the patient's sister nursed her, saw to her needs by day and night, tried to make her as comfortable as possible, scarcely ever left the house, was almost always at her bedside till the long, wearying, hopeless vigil was over.

One day, soon after the funeral, a friend said, " But how *could* you keep on day and night, month after month?"

The reply was, " Oh, it was easier than you might think. *You see, I knew we had such a little time left together.*"

Only a great love could make such a sacrifice.

SATURDAY—AUGUST 23.

I HOPE you'll forgive me for telling this story, but I'm sure every mother, and husband, will sympathise, with a smile!

A young mother-to-be was rushed to the maternity hospital, but just failed to reach the ward in time. Her baby was born in the lift! She was terribly embarrassed, and the nurses were doing their best to make her feel better.

" That's nothing to worry about," said one kindly. " Why, last year we'd a mother whose baby was actually born in the car park outside!"

At that the tears flooded forth again. " I know," sobbed the young mother. " That was me, too!"

SUNDAY—AUGUST 24.

A MERRY heart doeth good like a medicine.

THE FRIENDSHIP BOOK

HAVE you ever heard the story of Sir Foulk, the Welsh knight who attained great fame by his brave deeds during the Crusades. Stirred to envy his fellow knights scoffed every exploit with, " I could have done that as well as you."

Stung to retort, Sir Foulk challenged with twinkle in his eye, " I'll tell you something I can do and you can't—jump to the top of my castle." " We know your castle is the highest in Wales," they scoffed, " we won't believe you till we see you do it."

So he invited them all to dinner to witness the attempt. And afterwards he took them to the foot of the castle steps. " Watch me," he said, and, laughing, he jumped a step at a time till he had reached the top.

It was a lesson on what seemed impossible. We maybe can't fly to the top, but we can get there by taking a step at a time.

JILL is five and rather thoughtful. I like this story about her.

One day she sat on a stool in the kitchen listening to her mother and a neighbour talking about the awful weather. " And it's raining *again*," the neighbour declared.

" It always is !" Jill's mother replied.

Then a little voice said, " It was a lovely day yesterday."

Just a reminder that, often, even grown-ups get things wrong. It's very easy to forget the good and rail against the bad; very easy to minimise what is pleasant, and exaggerate what vexes or disappoints us.

WEDNESDAY—AUGUST 27.

IT'S good for a man to be taken down a peg now and again.

And perhaps no-one is better at doing it than his wife! This story will show you what I mean.

While peering at his reflection in the bathroom mirror before attending a Rotary dinner at which he was the guest speaker, a husband mused—"I wonder how many important members will be there?"

"One less than you think, dear," said his wife.

THURSDAY—AUGUST 28.

HERE are two recipes.

They'll never find their way into a cookery book, but I believe they should be on the menu for all of us. The first comes from Bill Shankly, the straightforward Scot who, for 14 years, has guided Liverpool Football Club to fame and fortune.

"When I retire," he said on his 59th birthday, "I'll get out my tracksuit and sweater and jog round the streets. People will laugh—but I'll die healthy!"

The other comes from Jack Benny, the comedian, now over 80. "Age," he said, "is strictly mind over matter!"

The years don't count if you're young in heart!

FRIDAY—AUGUST 29.

I NEVER see a sunset bright,
With flaming gold and red,
But what I've felt strange wonderment,
And to myself have said—
Grant, Lord, that I may live to see
Tomorrow's sun shine down on me.

SATURDAY—AUGUST 30.

IN a Glasgow hospital lay a little boy who was not at all well.

To help make up for all he was missing the nurses did their best. They noticed the stories he liked most were about the fire brigade, and the only toy he wanted to play with was a battered fire engine.

So the nurses had a word with the sister. Sister spoke to someone else. And eventually the story reached the firemaster himself. He called for volunteers for an extra-special display in their off-duty time. And when he explained why, every man stepped forward.

That's why, one day, a pale-faced little lad of six was wrapped up warmly and transported in style with a nurse and helper to the Central Fire Station in Ingram Street. Waiting for him, with gleaming helmets, shining boots and broad smiles, were the firemen, lined up beside their fire engines, with the firemaster himself in command. What a show they put on! They ran out hoses, made rescues from high windows with the turntable ladder, fought imaginary fires and manhandled heavy pumps. Afterwards he was shown the fire engines, allowed to hold a hose, and fitted with a fireman's hat.

And when it was all over, a fireman stepped forward and presented him with a super new toy fire engine, a memento of his visit.

Doesn't this story just make your day?

SUNDAY—AUGUST 31.

RECOMPENSE to no man evil for evil. If it be possible, as much as lieth in you, live peaceably with all men.

SEPTEMBER

MONDAY—SEPTEMBER 1.

I LIKE this homely Grace. I am told it first appeared in St Paul's, South Kensington, parish magazine :

Dear Lord, keep us from being like porridge, slow to boil and hard to stir, and make us like cornflakes, always prepared and ready to serve. Amen.

TUESDAY—SEPTEMBER 2.

A FRIEND of mine was visiting the children of the Royal Blind School in Edinburgh one afternoon. It was their sports period, and he watched the blind bairns playing cricket and football. Their football has a bell in it to guide the player and the batsman calls to the bowler, to let him know where to throw the outsize cricket ball. The batsman knows where it's going by the noise it makes when it bounces.

But my friend went on to say that when blind children run races the problem is to let them know where the tape is. So, as the starting pistol cracks, someone takes up a position behind the finishing tape with two flat pieces of wood—rather like the gadgets which Granny used to shape butter into pats. The two pieces of wood are clapped together, then the runners can judge not only where they've to go but how far they've to go to reach the tape !

These two clappers remind me of the courage and grit of handicapped people everywhere. Would we all rise to the challenge as bravely and cheerfully ?

THE FRIENDSHIP BOOK

WEDNESDAY—SEPTEMBER 3.

I SOMETIMES wish I hadn't done
What first came in my head.
I sometimes wish I'd done something —
Some kindly thing — instead.
I guess most of us wish that we
Were like the folk we WANT to be!

THURSDAY—SEPTEMBER 4.

LONG ago, certain tribes had a strange custom. If someone saved you from certain death, from that moment your life belonged to that person. I am reminded of this old custom when I think of Mrs Cathie Morrison, 145 Katrine Crescent, Kirkcaldy.

Cathie lay in hospital, stricken by a grave illness at the birth of her twins. The two bonnie little girls were fine. But Cathie's husband and parents were sent for and told there was little hope for her.

Yet the doctors worked all hours of the night and day to keep her alive, and she was rushed to Edinburgh, where another team of doctors was waiting to carry on the battle. It was another 24 hours before the first signs came that they were winning. Though nearly a year of poor health was to follow, I am glad to say that today, at 25, Cathie is her old self.

She was told that never before had anyone survived the crisis through which she passed, and though her simple thanks would have been enough, she chose to show her gratitude by taking up nursing, and though she has a young family to keep her busy, all her spare time is now given to nursing in a Kirkcaldy hospital.

Could those who triumphed in the fight to save her be rewarded in a richer way?

THE FRIENDSHIP BOOK

GRANDMA was lending a hand at bath-time.

Happily splashing together were David, who's five, Gordon, who's four, and their wee brother Tommy, who's 2½.

Grandma was chatting to Tommy as she washed behind his ears. " Imagine," she said, " there are three people in this bath tonight."

Tommy shook his head. " Only two," he said. "No, Tommy," smiled Grandma. " David's one, Gordon's two, and you're three !"

" I'm not three," retorted Tommy. " I'm only two and a half !"

D'you blame Grandma for giving up the struggle . . . ?

EVER heard of a bomb preaching a sermon?

James Lees, of Polwarth Grove, Edinburgh, told me about it. During the Second World War the Scots Kirk in Amsterdam was completely destroyed by a German bomb. The congregation, many of them Scots, determined it should be rebuilt.

Today, anyone who visits the kirk may be intrigued by the unusual offering plate at the door, a cone-shaped cup, mounted on a stand. It is the nose of the very bomb that destroyed the former church ! It had been found in the rubble.

Week by week the congregation place their offerings in it. The money is used not only for the upkeep of the church but to help in caring for unwanted children, for old folk, for those in trouble or despair, for the homeless, and many more.

So the symbol of death and destruction is now a symbol of forgiveness and faith.

SUNDAY—SEPTEMBER 7.

COME unto me, all ye that labour and are heavy laden, and I will give you rest.

MONDAY—SEPTEMBER 8.

BRENDA was a small girl who believed that she could pray for weather to suit her wishes. She had made great friends with people next door, who took her on their outings in the car. But, one day, when they were preparing to go it was obvious they were going to leave Brenda behind.

She started to cry, and the friends next door hearing her, relented. Brenda cried even louder. "What's wrong with you?" asked her mother. "You cried when you were not asked to the picnic and now you are crying even more when you are asked." Brenda sobbed, "But I've been praying for rain!"

Brenda would live to learn that prayer is not always asking. Sometimes it is listening to God's will.

TUESDAY—SEPTEMBER 9.

WHILE turning the pages of the life of a famous man—John Evelyn, who died in 1706—I came upon this tribute to him:

"He is well described as a patriot who kept his loyalty in dangerous times, a Christian who preserved his integrity in the most immoral, and a philosopher who viewed every object with a desire to extract from it all the beauty and goodness it contained."

The wording is somewhat old-fashioned, but the meaning is challengingly clear. I suggest that now and then you and I take time off to ask ourselves how we might live a little more finely.

G

WEDNESDAY—SEPTEMBER 10.

MARY, a Lancashire lass, suffers from disseminated sclerosis and is confined to bed or her wheeled chair.

Her great chum is Bosun, who lies and gazes up at her with adoring eyes, happy to serve in any way he can.

And this has prompted Mary to pass on to me a story of another dog who plays an important part in an American hospital for sick children. Sometimes some of the little patients are inclined to be weepy. Some go off their food. Some are suspicious as well as afraid.

Skeezer, a wise, well-trained " understanding" dog, wanders along to the cot where a frightened child is in tears or sullen, and just stands by, waiting to be patted and *talked to.* Sooner or later the child who wouldn't speak to anybody talks to Skeezer, and the child that had sat rigid and taut reaches out a timid little hand and strokes Skeezer's smooth head or gives him a gentle pat . . . and feels, deep down inside, he has at least one sympathetic friend in hospital.

And who should know more about these things than Mary?

THURSDAY—SEPTEMBER 11.

TOM THOMSON, of 17 Nile Street, Kirkcaldy, passes on this verse a friend has hanging in her kitchen.

Thank God for dirty dishes—they have a tale to tell; while other folk go hungry, they show we're eating well.

So even when the sink's piled high, please do not make a fuss; for by this stack of evidence, God's truly good to us.

FRIDAY—SEPTEMBER 12.

I OFTEN think some folk are mad—
Such silly things they do.
Such thoughtless things they say at times—
Such nonsense, in my view.
And then I pause—what if folk see
The same stupidity in me?

SATURDAY—SEPTEMBER 13.

A VERY loving granny, recently widowed, was sitting in her chair (she now lives with her married daughter) when Jean, aged six, began telling her about an outing she and the girl next door had enjoyed. " . . . and caught a bus, and were very careful, of course, and we went to the park, and we . . . Granny," she said, " you're not listening to me. You're thinking about Grandad !"

It was true.

That little accusation, gentle though it was, stabbed Granny wide awake. Jean means a great deal to her; and what Jean had said reminded her that she must try to be " with it," and not lose interest in folk about her. She must think about her man only when she was alone.

It isn't easy, but that is what the bereaved must try to do. Life becomes a challenge after a loved one has gone—a challenge to be interested in other people and their concerns, and somehow find healing for deep wounds, some joy in spite of great sorrow.

SUNDAY—SEPTEMBER 14.

WHAT doth the Lord require of thee, but to do justly, and to love mercy, and to walk humbly with thy God?

THE FRIENDSHIP BOOK

MONDAY—SEPTEMBER 15.

IF everybody was just like me,
What kind of world would this world be?

When I ask myself this I begin to feel hot under the collar and I lose any pomposity I may have. I see myself in a new light.

It is not a bad thing, to take a long, cool look at ourselves. It is so easy to be self-righteous and comfortably satisfied . . . and so easy to be blind to our own follies or much too ready to explain away our faults and make excuses for our behaviour.

The number of folk who have murdered somebody is comparatively small, but the number of near-saints who are prickly and awkward and difficult to live with is legion.

TUESDAY—SEPTEMBER 16.

NOT long before Sir Harry Lauder died, he learned of an old couple who, in the early days before his name was a household word, had toured the music halls with him. Now, lonely and forgotten in their tumbledown tenement home, life held little for them at the end of the road.

So Sir Harry drove to Glasgow and spent an hour or two with them, chatting about old times. A few weeks later the Rolls was at the door again. This time they were whisked off to Loch Lomond and stopped at the gate of a bonnie country cottage where a meal was ready for them.

" D'ye like it here?" queried Sir Harry. Their smiles gave him his answer. "Well," he said, " ye'll never hae tae leave it. It's a' yours." He had bought the cottage for them, and had set aside a handsome sum of money to ensure they would never want again as long as they lived.

There are not many like him.

THE FRIENDSHIP BOOK

I SOMETIMES feel life is unkind—
That somehow I must bear
Of pain or grief or daily ills
More than my rightful share.
But when I count my blessings—why,
How very fortunate am I!

LIKE many in late middle life, Sarah Smith lived alone, opening her door to nobody, venturing forth only for necessary messages and unknown to her neighbours. But when her half-pint of milk stood at the door for a whole day a neighbour knocked till she got Sarah to answer.

The result was that Sarah was rushed to hospital. It was a terrible ordeal for her, accustomed to living alone, and now in a ward of strangers. But she responded to the treatment and devoted nursing and began to take notice. She became interested in the other patients and responded shyly to their advances.

The first visiting day she expected nobody. But in walked the neighbour who had sent for the doctor. Other neighbours came, and at visiting times she was never alone. The almoner of the hospital arranged for her to apply for a supplementary pension and allowance for heating and lighting, as well as a rebate on her rent.

" I seem to matter to a lot of people," thought Sarah in astonished wonder. When she got home she found neighbours waiting to welcome her, and gladly she asked them in. Sarah had thought nobody cared for her friendship. She had to find out the hard way how wrong she was.

What a blessing good neighbours are!

FRIDAY—SEPTEMBER 19.

THE Lady of the House came home from the shops with a story.

It's about a man whose wife asked him to pop round to the greengrocer's for a cabbage. " What size?" he asked. " About as big as your head," she replied.

Ten minutes later he was back. His wife was delighted with the cabbage he brought. " Just right," she enthused. " However did you manage?"

" Simple," said her husband. " I just tried my hat on them all until I found one that fitted !"

SATURDAY—SEPTEMBER 20.

AT the end of a warm June day in 1882, Dr George Matheson, the blind minister of Innellan was alone in his manse, the rest of the family having gone to Glasgow for his sister's wedding. It was a perfect evening, but for the minister it was an evening of terrible despair. No one knows why, though some believe his sister's marriage brought back the memory of the day his fiancee broke their engagement because he'd gone blind.

In the depths of despair, something made him pick up his pen and begin to write. A short time later, four verses of a hymn lay before him :

> *O Love that wilt not let me go,*
> *I rest my weary soul in thee,*
> *I give thee back the life I owe,*
> *That in thine ocean depths its flow*
> *May richer, fuller be . . .*

These few minutes made him famous. For in this hymn, millions the world over have found comfort in their sorrow, strength in their weariness, and the faith to carry on through the worst that may befall.

SPIRIT OF THE HILLS

Just rock and snow, a prospect bare,
Yet climbing I find solace there,
And feel I'm near to Him who wills
The strength of these eternal hills.

DAVID HOPE

IN ROMAN DAYS

When the Romans fought in the heat of the sun
I'm sure they dreamed " When the war is done . . ."
I imagine them here, just everyday folk,
Enjoying a chat and a long hot soak.

DAVID HOPE

THE FRIENDSHIP BOOK

SUNDAY—SEPTEMBER 21.

THEY that wait upon the Lord shall renew their
strength.

MONDAY—SEPTEMBER 22.

NOT long ago a friend of mine had to stay for a
few days with her mum who had taken ill.

That meant her husband had to look after their
six-year-old boy on his own.

Just as Dad was tucking him up that night, the
small son remarked, " I shall miss Mummy."

Sweet little thing, his father thought fondly,
and asked, " Why's that ?"

" Well," said the little chap, " she won't be
here to do up the top button on my shirt in the
morning."

I somehow think that's not the only reason she'd
be missed.

TUESDAY—SEPTEMBER 23.

THE Lady of the House paused, a postage stamp
in one hand and an envelope in the other.

" I wonder," she murmured, " how many stamps
we've used in our lifetime."

A stamp, whatever its value, is no more than a
tiny scrap of flimsy paper. What we pay for is not
the stamp but the service we get. Without a stamp
on the envelope a letter from Liverpool to London
might cost quite a bit; and how should we receive a
letter from Australia ?

There came to mind that shrewd comment by
Josh Billings, " *Consider the postage stamp, my son.
Its usefulness consists in its ability to stick to one
thing till it gets there.*"

Something of a virtue, surely?

WEDNESDAY—SEPTEMBER 24.

IT'S sad to see the summer pass,
To feel the autumn's chill,
And watch the early sundown draw
Night over roof and hill.
But, don't forget, though no birds sing,
Soon, soon again will come the spring.

THURSDAY—SEPTEMBER 25.

I WONDER if you have heard of the cathedral of the trees. It stands on a hilltop in Glencruitten, not far from Oban, and though it is many years since I last visited it, I shall never forget it.

The outline of the cathedral is marked by a double wall of chestnut and lime trees. The entrance is formed by two evergreens, trimmed in the shape of an archway. The pillars are of yew, the altar is clothed with cotoneaster, and above it stands a golden yew, clipped to form a cross. Instead of paving, the cathedral is carpeted with heaths, and in place of stained glass windows are trees with foliage of purple, crimson and copper and every shade of green.

It was the dream of Alexander Mackay, whose home was at Glencruitten. He began to plant the cathedral in 1921, knowing he would never see it completed, for he was already an old man, and it would take fifty years for the trees to grow to maturity and reveal the cathedral in its true splendour. When he died in 1934 he was buried there, beside the altar.

In time his wife, his only son and, recently, his great-grandson, Ferrier, were laid to rest there, too, in the family's unique memorial, a living cathedral.

There could be no lovelier resting-place.

FRIDAY—SEPTEMBER 26.

THE greatest of all Norwegian musicians was undoubtedly Edvard Grieg, whose great-grandfather was a Scotsman.

This gifted son of Norway had a hard fight for recognition. He was scorned by many who ought to have known better, and the gallant fight went on till Liszt, the famous Hungarian composer, gave him a word of praise and declared that Grieg's *Piano Concerto* deserved immortality. That assurance gave the younger man the courage he needed till fame came to him.

Every day we are influencing for good or ill those about us. Indifference or criticism can wound and depress. But kindness, patience and encouragement can bring out the best. Try it!

SATURDAY—SEPTEMBER 27.

SOMETHING in a letter from Mrs Norah Duncan, of St Paul, Minnesota, can help us all.

Mrs Duncan's brother fought in the 1914 to 1918 war. It was trench warfare, and after a spell " at the front " there was the march back to rest billets, often a long way behind the lines.

What agony those marches were—the wet uniforms, the heavy weapons, the big boots coated with mud . . . Every yard was misery for the men. Some just gave in—dropping by the roadside. But this soldier kept plodding on. " I can take twenty-five steps more," he told himself. Then another twenty-five steps, then twenty, fifteen, ten, five till at last it was one step more, one step more till he arrived in the billets and dropped asleep on the floor.

Keep telling yourself you can carry on for a wee bit yet—and you'll conquer life's toughest roads.

SUNDAY—SEPTEMBER 28.

SEEK ye the Lord while he may be found, call ye upon him while he is near.

MONDAY—SEPTEMBER 29.

I HEARD of a minister who began a sermon declaring that he'll never attend another football match. That made his congregation sit up —and then, with a wry smile the minister gave seven reasons:

1. Every time he went to a match somebody asked him for money.

2. He used to go faithfully every week, but the manager never visited him.

3. The seats were too hard.

4. Nobody ever spoke to him.

5. The referee made decisions with which he couldn't agree.

6. Since he bought a book on football he can sit at home and read it, or watch the game on TV. He considers himself as good a fan as the people who go faithfully every week, and pay.

7. Saturday afternoon's the only time he has off —and a man's got to have some time to himself, after all!

His congregation soon saw what he was getting at—and I'm sure it didn't take *you* long!

TUESDAY—SEPTEMBER 30.

HOLD fast when come life's ills and fears,
When sorrow's shadows fall,
When hope is gone and you are crushed,
And see no light at all.
Clouds gather in your sky and mine—
But, after rain, the sun must shine.

OCTOBER

WEDNESDAY—OCTOBER 1.

ROBERT ANDERSON, of Anstruther, was telling me a story the other day.

When he was a boy, he would come in at lunchtime and ask what was for dinner, to be given the answer : " Manners."

He told me he was almost grown-up before he realised that " Manners " wasn't a special dish, but simply a reminder it wasn't manners to ask ! Some people may feel that manners are not very important, but what a difference they make to everyday living!

THURSDAY—OCTOBER 2.

THERE are few Christians in the English-speaking world who have not heard the name of William Barclay of Glasgow University. His lectures and broadcasts are popular with old and young alike. His books have been translated into a score of languages and the number of copies published runs into millions.

It all began some years ago, when the Church of Scotland was in need of a new handbook on a certain subject. Dr J. W. Stevenson, remarking that " there was a minister in Renfrew called Barclay, who is rather good at that sort of thing," wrote a letter asking Barclay if he would be willing to undertake this small task. He was not thought of as more than a stopgap.

How many talented people are hidden away in Renfrew or Reigate, in Ratho or Rugby, and, like Professor Barclay, need only to be given the opportunity to show their talents?

FRIDAY—OCTOBER 3.

THE long, light evenings now are gone.
Alone, alone I sit.
Half-hoping somebody will come
And chat with me a bit.
Will no one raise the latch and say—
" Now, dearie, how are you today?"

SATURDAY—OCTOBER 4.

IN my newspaper recently I counted 41 announcements of deaths.

At the end of 13 were the words — " No letters, please." And I found myself thinking about something a doctor friend had said.

Time and again he has seen the comfort letters of sympathy can bring. Often they recall small incidents which a husband or wife never even thought of mentioning at home, but which left a deep and lasting impression on someone else— so much so that, years later, they are still remembered with gratitude.

It may seem letters of sympathy only deepen the pain of parting. Yet my friend assures me that he has known them to be a lifeline, helping the bereaved to meet life more bravely. He tells me how such letters become treasured possessions, for when a loved one is gone, every memory, however small, becomes infinitely more precious.

That is why it saddens the doctor to see those three words, " No letters, please," and I must say I am inclined to agree.

SUNDAY—OCTOBER 5.

FEAR God, and keep his commandments : for this is the whole duty of man.

THE FRIENDSHIP BOOK

MRS LORNA HILL, of Brockleside, Keswick, told me that when her mother was a girl in her teens, she used to write verses for Christmas cards. The family had little money to spare, and the money she earned was a godsend.

One day, Edith was asked to put a poem to a picture of a child with its mother, head bowed and hands folded. She wrote three simple verses, and was paid 5s for them.

But forty years later she read four lines in a newspaper. No one knew who had written them, but Edith Leatham recognised them as her own work, one verse of that five-shilling poem of long ago.

And before she died, in 1939, she saw them travel the world as perhaps the most perfect prayer for children that has ever been written.

Thank you for the world so sweet,
Thank you for the food we eat,
Thank you for the birds that sing,
Thank you, God, for everything.

THE Rev. Dr Stalker of Aberdeen was noted in his prayers for thanking God for a bright and sunny day whenever it occurred. On one particularly blustery and snowy night, two elders were walking to church. " Well, there is one thing sure, the doctor won't be thanking God for the weather tonight," said one, and the other nodded agreement.

But when the service began, the first petition of Dr Stalker's prayer was, " Oh, God, we thank thee that the weather is not always like this." It is cheering to think that even the dullest day can have its bright side—if only in contrast.

THE FRIENDSHIP BOOK

*HOW hard it is to suffer, and
To try not to complain.
But harder still to see through tears
A loved one grey with pain.
If this should be your lot, may you
Have strength and courage to come through.*

I WONDER if the title of a book published last century means anything to you? It is *Granny's Wonderful Chair*. It was a favourite with children for generations ; and when it had been out of print for 23 years it was rewritten by the American writer, Frances Hodgson Burnett, under the title *Stories From the Lost Fairy Book*. The author of *Granny's Wonderful Chair* was blind. She was one of the 12 children of the postmaster in a Donegal village. As a child, Frances knew only poverty. Her days were filled with chores. At night she dreamed dreams and lived in a bright world of fancy. She had to have others to tell her stories and to write her poems and tales for her ; and she earned a few pennies when her songs were published in the *Irish Penny Journal*.

Eventually the blind lassie moved to Edinburgh, and had an income from the Royal Bounty Fund of £20. Her health was poor, but she and her sister (who was eyes to the blind) moved to London, after a gift of £100 from the Marquess of Lansdowne.

All her life—from 1816 to 1887—she lived in a fairyland of her own making; and her collection of stories became world famous, and a treasured possession of almost every girl. Does it not all go to show that something dwells in each of us that can make us stronger than our surroundings?

FRIDAY—OCTOBER 10.

THE Lady of the House's grocer is something of a wag.

" Morning, Mrs Gay," he grinned as she came into the shop. " Why did Adam and Eve have an ideal marriage ?"

The Lady of the House smiled back and confessed she'd no idea.

" Because," said the grocer with a twinkle in his eye, " he didn't have to listen to her stories about all the men she could have married — and she didn't have to listen to his about his mother's cooking !"

SATURDAY—OCTOBER 11.

THE highest wall of our garden has been aglow this year, for in a wrought-iron hay rack, partly filled with soil held in by moss, were a variety of trailing geraniums and blue lobelia among small green and yellow leaves.

A year or two ago, the Lady of the House received from Mrs Hilda Drew of Bognor Regis a gift of a few miniature roses together with two wee sprays of fern. When the roses had died the fern was still fresh so I poked the bits into the hay rack. Imagine my delight when the snippets rooted.

Since then Mrs Drew has passed on. We miss the friendly letters she sent, but we cannot forget her, for throughout summer and winter the delicate yellowy-green fern reminds us of a kind and gracious lady who lived to do good.

SUNDAY—OCTOBER 12.

A SOFT answer turneth away wrath.

MONDAY—OCTOBER 13.

WHEN I was just a little girl
The best time of each day
Was when I snuggled down in bed,
And Mum would come and say:
" A bedtime story, love?" She'd read
Until I said my prayers —
Then kiss me once or twice before
She softly crept downstairs.
Now I'M a mum with children three
I do just what she did for me!

TUESDAY—OCTOBER 14.

WHEN John died suddenly early in 1971, Margaret sold her house and most of her furniture. She put the remainder in store and went to live with her married son and his family.

She told us the other evening that it had all been a great mistake. " I wanted to escape from the house that spoke of John," she explained. " Recalling the past hurt so much. I just couldn't get away from the house or the neighbourhood quickly enough.

" But that first morning in my son's house in the South of England! I walked down the street and nobody knew me. I realised then that I had done the wrong thing.

" My son and his wife could not have been kinder, but it didn't work out. The noise, the fuss, the children—bless them!—getting on my nerves; my own furniture crowded into a small room — no privacy, no friends—it almost broke my heart. I had to come back. It was a big wrench, but now I feel happier . . . and nearer to John. I can take flowers to the cemetery. Having to go to work is hard, and yet a blessing; and my needs are few. I began trying to build a new life too soon . . . much too soon! "

WEDNESDAY—OCTOBER 15.

I HAVE noticed more and more in recent years that the custom of Harvest Thanksgiving in the churches is tending to change. We have fewer bags of potatoes, sheaves of corn, and untrimmed turnips. More and more it is the children who bring neatly-packaged parcels of fruit or flowers which are later distributed by these same children to the old folk throughout the town or to those in hospital.

So it comes about that many an old-age pensioner hears her doorbell ring on a Sunday afternoon and opens it to find two or three young people there with a gift of honey, or fresh farm eggs, or jam. And I'm sure that what thrills the pensioner is not the value of the gift, but just that he or she is remembered, just to see these bright and smiling faces. It may be a platitude to say it, but it really is the thought that counts !

THURSDAY—OCTOBER 16.

AN American, on a visit to India, went to meet an elderly woman missionary. When he saw the woman waiting to greet him, he halted, stared and exclaimed, " Why, you sure are beautiful !"

" Of course," said his smiling hostess. " I'm seventy-four !"

What I like about this story is the, " Of course !" Surely a reminder to all that whatever they do when young is reflected in their looks when old. A life of being helpful, kindly, gracious and serene should give them an appeal that youth can never supply.

I venture to say every woman over fifty should look more beautiful than ever . . . if only she lives rightly, is happy at heart and does not fear growing old !

H

FRIDAY—OCTOBER 17.

IF one you loved has now passed on,
How sad for you, and yet
How glad you'll be you never spoke
A word you now regret.
How thankful you must be today
For unkind words you didn't say.

SATURDAY—OCTOBER 18.

MARGARET, of Glasgow, has no need to leave home ten minutes early in the morning.

But by doing so, she has time to pop across the street, open Mrs Ritchie's door, put the electric kettle on, make a cup of tea, and take it into Mrs Ritchie's bedroom.

For the last four years Margaret has done that five mornings a week — she arrives a wee bit later on Saturday and Sunday. She also enjoys doing a bit of shopping for Mrs Ritchie, and when she delivers the goods she sits down for a chat.

Very kind, very thoughtful, very sweet of Margaret, only 22. But if you said so, she would smile, and explain that her mother died when she was only five, and that Mrs Ritchie used to take her to school every morning, and meet her every afternoon, and make beautiful little dresses, and take her walks in the country, and remember every birthday that came along!

So doing little things for her now, Margaret would explain, is really nothing much . . .

SUNDAY—OCTOBER 19.

THE Lord seeth not as man seeth: for man looketh on the outward appearance, but the Lord looketh on the heart.

MONDAY—OCTOBER 20.

ONE day Rabbi Gamaliel sent his housekeeper to buy the best meat she could find.

When the evening meal was served, the housekeeper set a delicious tongue before her master.

Some weeks later the Rabbi asked her to buy the worst meat she could find. "The very worst," he emphasised. "I am making an experiment."

For the evening meal, the housekeeper served tongue again. Smiling, she explained: "Master, there is nothing better than a good tongue, and nothing worse than a bad one."

It is an old story, reminding us that a bad tongue can cause untold misery and that a good tongue can be a blessing and a comfort to all.

TUESDAY—OCTOBER 21.

ONE of the sweetest and bravest lassies I know is Tommy's wife, Margaret, who lives in County Durham. Her hubby is far from well, there is not a lot of money coming in, and Margaret has to plan her budget and manage along as best she can. Her own health leaves a lot to be desired, but for years she has done things for others.

Quite recently in the local post office Margaret noticed an old body trying to fill in a form. The pen wasn't all that good ; neither were the old body's eyes. She fumbled.

Margaret stepped forward and helped the old body, filled in the form, showed her where to sign her name, and then to her astonishment found her hands held warmly. "Eh, dearie," said a grateful woman, "what lovely hands you've got . . . so beautiful and soft *and kind* !"

That gave Margaret a new lease of life and cheered her no end.

WEDNESDAY—OCTOBER 22.

I WAS going out to pick some blackberries the other week, but the Lady of the House shook her head. "We haven't had a touch of frost yet," she said. Two days later she told me over the breakfast table, "There was frost last night. You can pick your blackberries now."

I did and they were lovely. Full and glistening and with that extra sharp tang an early frost seems to give them. Some of the flowers in the garden, too, seemed all the brighter for their nip of Jack Frost. My cornflowers were a more vivid blue than before.

Isn't it the same with ourselves ? A friend strikes a bad patch, goes through a spell of trouble. In a mysterious way the experience enriches him so that he comes out of the crisis strengthened by what has passed, his faith not shaken but wonderfully renewed.

THURSDAY—OCTOBER 23.

FATHER'S DAY has come and gone. But I feel I must pass on these lines entitled simply "A Prayer for Father on Father's Day," and signed George Petrie, aged 15. I can't help feeling George's Dad must be an exceptional man to have prompted such a fine tribute :

Mender of toys, leader of boys,
Changer of fuses, kisser of bruises,
Bless him, O Lord.
Mover of couches, soother of ouches,
Pounder of nails, teller of tales,
Reward him, O Lord.
Raker of leaves, cleaner of eaves,
Drier of dishes, fulfiller of wishes,
Bless him, O Lord . . .

FRIDAY—OCTOBER 24.

"AYE, you get them!" said the street cleaner, urging the last leaf into a neat pile. "Mrs Smith comes down the road this morning and says, 'My, what a mess those leaves have made!' Then along comes Mrs Wilson and says, 'Good morning, don't the leaves look lovely!'

"Well, I swept them up, and along comes Mrs Smith again. 'You're wasting your time,' says she. 'The wind will have them away again in a minute.' But Mrs Wilson said, 'My, you've made a lovely job of the street! It looks so tidy now!'"

I suppose it depends how you look at things.

SATURDAY—OCTOBER 25.

MRS VIOLET MOSS, of Prospect Road, Stafford, tells me that she and her daughter and her wee grandson share a very simple faith. Mrs Moss has not had an easy life, but somehow she has kept smiling because she has a genius for trusting things to work out for the best.

In her letter to me she says, "It is a good thing to have faith in God when we are bewildered and troubled. It is also a good thing to have faith in God when all goes well."

How true it is. God is not just somebody to run to when we are afraid or in desperate need. He is a friend with whom we should share our joys as much as our sorrows; and the true Christian—and Mrs Moss is one—shares her joys and sorrows with God, and (as the Bible puts it) walks every day with the Lord she loves.

Many folk today scorn such a simple faith. But the fact is that all who have such a faith are radiantly happy when all goes well, and have an inward source of calm repose when life is unkind.

SUNDAY—OCTOBER 26.

GOD is our refuge and strength, a very present help in trouble.

MONDAY—OCTOBER 27.

SOME years ago as Annie was leaving her church after morning worship something caught her attention. It was the table of hymn books by the door and it was untidy. Annie always brought her own hymn book, but she knew that some of the congregation borrowed one from the table and so, of course, did the occasional visitor. Anyway, the untidiness offended Annie's eye and she soon had the books in neat piles.

Every Sunday since Annie has stopped by the table to tidy up the books. She never leaves the church without doing it. Not much in that, you may think. Anybody could do it. Yes, but only Annie does.

TUESDAY—OCTOBER 28.

RUTH GOODES, of St Peters, South Australia, was telling us about Stephanie, who is four, and small for her age. One afternoon Stephanie went into a shop to buy ice-cream. She was a long time there, and Mother went in to see what was keeping her. It turned out that, as Stephanie's so small, nobody saw her on the other side of the counter!

So that night, when her father came home, he got to work, and next day presented Stephanie with a notice at the end of a short pole. On it were these words : " Please serve me—I'm down here !"

Wee Stephanie now gets instant service—and with a smile, too !

WEDNESDAY—OCTOBER 29.

I THINK, if I grow very old,
And find life hard to bear,
I will not dwell on daily ills
Or be cast down by care.
Instead of age's grief and pain,
I'll dream up youth's sweet thrills again!

THURSDAY—OCTOBER 30.

ROY SUTHERLAND, of Newbattle, Edinburgh, shares with me from time to time the gems which come from children at Sunday school.

Roy had just told his class the story of the prodigal son. He asked them if they could tell him who wasn't pleased when the prodigal returned, expecting someone to say immediately, "The elder brother."

No one spoke. There were puzzled looks, and shuffling of feet. "Come on," Roy prompted. "Have a guess!"

At which one wee lad put up his hand and declared: "The fatted calf!"

FRIDAY—OCTOBER 31.

WHAT'S the time on your clock? I know a jeweller's shop where every clock and every watch has its hands set at ten minutes to two. Why? Because Alex., who runs the business with his wife Anna, feels it gives the shop a happier atmosphere.

Clocks with hands at ten to two look as if they're wearing a smile, says Alex. Clocks with hands at twenty-five past seven give a short of down-in-the mouth, disgruntled look.

So make sure that your clock is set at ten to two!

NOVEMBER

SATURDAY—NOVEMBER 1.

I AM wondering if anybody now remembers one of the rarest spirits and greatest men of all time. His statue is in the island of Formosa where, 200 years ago, lived a hill tribe of headhunters.

The Chinese, dwelling in the plains, lived in terror of the headhunters, but could not stop their raids. At last they sent a Chinese up to the hill. His name was Gaw Hong, and he had immense courage, also a wonderfully friendly nature. For some odd reason he was not decapitated, but lived among the headhunters, learned their language, became their friend, and at last persuaded them to give up their cruel practice of headhunting.

But the day came when they explained to Gaw Hong that their greatest feast was due to take place, and instead of raiding the lowlands, they were willing to sacrifice one head only. Gaw Hong tried to persuade them to change their minds, but he failed. " Well, then," he said at last, " you take one head only. Tomorrow morning, kill the first traveller who comes along the hill track— a man in a brown coat and a red hat."

Next morning a man in a brown coat and a red hat came at dawn along the appointed path, he was clubbed—and only when he lay dead did they recognise their friend, Gaw Hong.

That was in 1769—and that day headhunting ceased in Formosa.

SUNDAY—NOVEMBER 2.

THE disciple is not above his master : but every one that is perfect shall be as his master.

THE FRIENDSHIP BOOK

MONDAY—NOVEMBER 3.

I WAS watching " Songs Of Praise " on TV from St George's Tron Kirk in Glasgow.

During the singing of that fine hymn, " Thine Be The Glory," the cameras, which usually pick out faces among the congregation, focused instead on the hands of a young woman in the choir. I was mystified until I realised she was blind and she was " reading " her Braille hymnal with her hands. As the camera moved up, we saw her face was aglow with joy. Indeed, you could hear her clear soprano voice soaring above the others.

Margaret Houston lives in Netherplace Road, Glasgow, and she possesses one of the biggest hymn books in Scotland. What can normally fit between the covers of one slim volume fills four bulky volumes in Braille writing. To you and me, the millions of raised dots are meaningless. But to Margaret, they spell out a message of faith and triumph.

TUESDAY—NOVEMBER 4.

THE apple is an annual temptation to small boys in the fruit season.

But most of us will feel sympathy for the young policeman who chased some boys plundering an orchard and, catching one of them, shut him in the police-box until he told him the names of the other boys.

Of course, even in the days when officialdom was less controlled in what it could and could not do, he had to let him out. As he ran off, the boy shouted, " And I didn't tell you their names. *And I ate your supper in the box!*"

It raises a smile, with the reflection on how difficult the life of the man on the beat can be.

WEDNESDAY—NOVEMBER 5.

MARIANNE MACDONALD, of British Columbia, tells us of a little girl brought with her family to a relief camp set up in a disaster area. They were homeless and starving. For days they'd barely enough to stay alive, and every scrap and morsel had to be shared.

Gently, one of the nurses knelt beside the thin, ragged child, and held out a glass of milk. Wide-eyed, the little girl looked at it. Then she whispered, " How deep may I drink ?"

The nurse had tears in her eyes as she put her arm round that starving waif and said, " You can drink as deep as you like."

THURSDAY—NOVEMBER 6.

WORRY is like a rocking-chair—gives you something to do but doesn't get you anywhere.

FRIDAY—NOVEMBER 7.

LOOKING closely at the badge in my friend's jacket, I read, " Thanks Badge." It had the Scout emblem in the centre, and he told me that this badge is awarded to those who have given of their time and energies to the Scout movement, without being a uniformed member.

Sometimes we are grateful to people and don't know how to show our appreciation to them. The Scouts have come up with their answer to a long-felt need. We can't all hand out badges, but we can say, " Thank you," in many different ways.

A bunch of flowers, a little gift or even just a letter in gratitude.

Such actions are appreciated more than you ever know.

SATURDAY—NOVEMBER 8.

GEORDIE FRASER says thank you 156 times a day!

Geordie is a pensioner living in a one-roomed tenement flat, just off Victoria Road, Aberdeen. Twenty years ago, Geordie lost a leg. Difficult for any man to cope with, but for Geordie even more so, for he lives alone.

He discovered what a blessing good neighbours can be. One brought in his coal and lit his fire. Another went for his groceries. Someone else cleaned his windows and gave him a hand with the housework, and others just popped in to sit with him and chat for a while. How Geordie longed to be able to say "thank you" in some way. But how?

Then one neighbour mentioned her clock had stopped. Geordie said he'd be pleased to have a look at it. And, hey presto, in next to no time it was going again, its chime ringing out merrily for the first time in years. Word of Geordie's prowess spread, and other neighbours brought their clocks in, for every home seems to have its silent clock. The result is, not a week passes but Geordie repairs two or three clocks for neighbours or friends, and soon they're ticking and chiming as good as new.

Why 156 "thank you's"? Simply because every day a clock gives 156 chimes—and with every chime, it's as if Geordie is saying, with his broad and genial smile—"Thank you for all you've done for me."

SUNDAY—NOVEMBER 9.

BE strong and of a good courage; be not afraid, neither be thou dismayed: for the Lord thy God is with thee, wheresoever thou goest.

THE family had been having a rough time. The wife's mother was ill, the husband had been off work ; and, to crown all, their son had just sailed for Australia, where he was to be married. His parents would dearly have liked to go to the wedding, but they just couldn't see their way to getting there.

Then a cousin in Australia stepped in. " Come over at my expense," he said. " Be my guest. It won't cost you a penny."

They tell me their son was quite overcome when he saw them. It was a joyful reunion, and after the wedding there was a long holiday before it was time to fly home again, feeling fresh and fit and very grateful.

However much the trip cost the generous donor, it was worth every penny.

TUESDAY—NOVEMBER 11.

" NOTHING except a battle lost can be half so melancholy as a battle won." So said the Duke of Wellington, surely one of the very greatest soldiers who ever lived. And we can imagine that as he spoke these words he was looking upon the serried ranks of slain and injured. We can imagine that he was thinking not only of the slaughter in the day which had just passed, but of the coarsening of men's lives ; of the women left without husbands and children left fatherless.

It is more than a century and a half since he spoke these words, and all the time the business of war has been growing more deadly and more dangerous. Can our leaders, can the people not see that in modern war there can be no winners— only losers among the ruins ?

THE FRIENDSHIP BOOK

THE dreams for which young heroes died,
How cheap they seem today —
Except to those who loved so much,
And watched them march away.
We live because they died, and yet
They live if we do not forget!

THERE'S scarcely a leaf left on any tree in our neighbourhood now. But in Tarland, Aberdeenshire, I heard of a tree on which leaves are unfolding every week—even though we are well into winter!

It all started when the children in the Sunday school there learned that a missionary in Malawi was trying to start a new orchard. Of course, money was needed to buy the young saplings to plant out, and money was short. So the children decided they'd help out by washing dishes, cleaning cars, going for errands, helping Mum in the house and Dad in the garden, and then send out their wages to the missionaries.

To keep track of how much they sent, they had drawn a big tree on a piece of paper—just the trunk and branches, but no leaves. The idea was that for every 5p they raised the children stuck another leaf on the tree.

As I say, the leaves grew thick and fast on the Tarland tree and, as a result, the orchard in Malawi gradually filled up with row upon row of orange and lemon trees, which one day will provide fruit for undernourished children.

That's the story of the tree that grows leaves in winter—and I'm sure you'll agree it's a splendid idea.

FRIDAY—NOVEMBER 14.

LIFE on a newspaper can be hectic.

Often there isn't much time, and if a piece of paper lands on the floor instead of the wastepaper basket, no one's going to stop and pick it up. So, at the end of the day, you can imagine the office cleaner has a lot to do.

One Friday night, at the end of a hard week, things were a lot worse than usual when little Mrs Thompson came in. A friend of mine who was still at his desk apologised. " I'm afraid we're an untidy lot in here," he added.

" Oh, well," said Mrs T. with a shake of her head, " if you didn't make a mess, I wouldn't have a job."

You don't expect to find a philosopher wearing an apron and wielding a brush—but I fancy a touch of Mrs T.'s outlook could help us all through the day's problems.

SATURDAY—NOVEMBER 15.

DO these lines hold a challenge for you, as well as a smile ?

> He was a very cautious man
>> Who never romped or played.
> He never laughed. He never dreamed,
>> Nor kissed a pretty maid.
> So when he passed away, they say
>> Insurance was denied,
> For since he never really lived,
>> They claim he never died !

SUNDAY—NOVEMBER 16.

HAVE we not all one father? Hath not one God created us?

INSPIRATION

When the sky is darkest
Faith can burn most bright,
Pushing back the shadows
With its eternal light.

DAVID HOPE

A DAY TO REMEMBER

*The sun on your back
And the sea at your feet;
Simple pleasures
That make life sweet . . .*

The song of the waves
Slipping into the bay,
The signature tune
Of a wonderful day.

DAVID HOPE

NEWS! NEWS!

Don't hesitate to share it
And pass it round about;
Good news is welcome any time,
Declare it with a shout!

DAVID HOPE

THE FRIENDSHIP BOOK

DO you ever look at a blanket and see a miracle? Imagine you've survived an earthquake in Morocco. Your home has disappeared. You have no food, no place to go. You are tired and cold. Then someone hands you a clean, new blanket. He's also handed you comfort, warmth and shelter. Surely in such circumstances a blanket is a miracle.

I heard of a wee house at 192 Clydesdale Street, New Stevenston, which had produced 100 such miracles. It's there that little Mrs Elizabeth Watt lives. She's been a widow for years and I don't suppose she'll mind if I tell you she is over 90. Every year for 25 years she knitted four blankets for the Red Cross. I've no idea how many stitches you need for a blanket. But I do know it's an awful lot of care and compassion.

THIS story is about Tom, a tall, dark and hand-some bridegroom, and one of the kindest lads you could find. At the wedding reception, the bride's father said little about his daughter, Helen, but told two stories about Tom.

When only six, Tom had gone to a flower show and taken home a flower for his Mum. " As Tom couldn't afford to buy flowers," said the speaker, " he picked up a flower from the dustbin near a stall . . . and his mother valued it because she knew love had prompted the deed."

The second story was of Tom, aged 26. " He was up before seven this morning," said Helen's father, " away into town to buy flowers for his mum. And I am sure of one thing—if he's as kind to my daughter as he has always been to his mother . . . well, it's going to be a happy marriage."

WEDNESDAY—NOVEMBER 19.

*Y*OU *doubt if you can do this thing,*
And see the task right through?
You're too afraid to start? Perhaps
The job's too big for you?
Take courage, friend: begin, keep on,
No matter what the plan.
You CAN do it if only you
Make up your mind you can!

THURSDAY—NOVEMBER 20.

MRS SARAH BROWN, of Slamannan, was one of ten children. Her father, a miner, was cycling to work one day forty years ago when he met a friend who worked in Coats's thread mill in Paisley. He gave Sarah's father an outsize reel of black thread.

Well, that reel of thread was a godsend, for you can imagine the clothes that had to be sewn for four boys and six girls. Later, when all four laddies joined their father in the pits, there were moleskin trousers, waistcoats and caps to be made. It helped to make suits and skirts for the girls, it sewed on buttons, it was brought out every time clothes were handed down. Hardly a day passed but that reel was in use.

That was forty years ago. Today, both Sarah's parents are dead. Two girls are nursing in Greenock. Eight of the family still live in Slamannan, one unmarried sister in their old home, where all still visit. And that reel of black thread is still in use! It's like one of the family—a bit worn, perhaps, and a bit older, but there when it's needed.

No wonder it stands as proud as a trophy. For its strands have been woven into the very pattern of their lives.

FRIDAY—NOVEMBER 21.

IN the days when they seem to have been fond of leaving conditions to their wills, a father directed that his fortune should be left to the one of his three sons who should most successfully fill a room with anything that cost only a shilling.

One son tried to fill it with bricks and only managed half-full. The second bought straw, the cheapest thing he could think of and only succeeded in filling it three-quarters. But the third son bought a candle and filled the whole room with light.

SATURDAY—NOVEMBER 22.

EVEN if you try to shut your ears it is difficult not to overhear conversation in a bus.

As I found when two women were discussing bringing up their families, how much they needed in new clothes and shoes, the cost of feeding them and their constant asking for more pocket-money. The bus echoed with complaints and grumbles.

Until a woman sitting in front turned and spoke :

" I couldn't help hearing what you said. I used to be like that. My boy was a great expense, too. We had to sacrifice to give him what he needed."

Then she paused as tears came to her eyes.

" But then he died. Now he doesn't cost us anything but, oh, I would give the world to have him back again."

There was a silence that could be felt, but each one of us was thinking our own thoughts.

SUNDAY—NOVEMBER 23.

AS ye would that men should do to you, do ye also to them likewise.

MONDAY—NOVEMBER 24.

ONE sentence in a book I have been reading challenges me: "Self-pity is the furnace where everything gets melted down and wasted."

How very true this is! It means that however much you have suffered mentally and physically, whatever poverty, grief, disappointment and misfortune has done to your life, keeping on being sorry for yourself and nursing a grudge against circumstances achieves just nothing. The good as well as the evil is destroyed.

So if you feel your life has been an utter and undeserved failure, I would say: The less you dwell on the past and the sooner you try to plan a better future, the more likely you are to struggle out of the darkness of the past into the warm light of tomorrow.

TUESDAY—NOVEMBER 25.

HOW often we find that the greatest of men are the most humble. When the Rev. Dr John Fraser was Moderator of the General Assembly of the Church of Scotland he travelled to London to attend a luncheon. He had as a fellow guest the Rev. " Tubby " Clayton, who became famous as the founder of Toc H. of whom I have written before. As they emerged from the hall, " Tubby " said to the Moderator, " We have enjoyed our fellowship together and it has been a happy time. To make it complete, will you give me your blessing ?"

And there and then in the middle of London on the dusty street, he knelt down to receive the Moderator's blessing. Ever afterwards Dr Fraser recalled it as the most moving experience of his year of office.

WEDNESDAY—NOVEMBER 26.

P LEASE do a little kindness —
Take someone by surprise;
Set some sad heart a-dancing,
Put laughter in old eyes.
So nice to bless somebody
(It doesn't matter who);
And making someone happy
Will make YOU happy, too!

THURSDAY—NOVEMBER 27.

"*MARY had a little lamb*" is a rhyme known to children everywhere, but have you ever wondered who Mary was?

Well, Mary's father was a shepherd in the Welsh hills and often came home after a stormy night with weak or sick lambs to be looked after. His daughter Mary would take them until they were able to look after themselves. Two of these lambs were her special pets, and she named them Billy and Nell. Soon they were following her everywhere, watching her from the farm gate every morning as she left for school, and waiting when she came home. Once, Billy managed to escape, and to the teacher's dismay he turned up in the classroom.

This story became known throughout Llangollen, and a few years later a visitor from London heard all about it from Mary herself. That visitor, Jane Buell, wrote stories and rhymes for children— and before long, she'd turned Billy's escapade into five short verses.

Today it's one of the best-known nursery rhymes in the world. When Mary was an old lady of 87, she confessed that to hear her story on the lips of so many children was one of the great joys of her life.

FRIDAY—NOVEMBER 28.

DON'T pretend life is always a beautiful song,
Or the sky's always blue as can be;
For clouds can loom up on a warm summer day,
With dark shadows for you and for me.
But never forget that the stormiest night
Can lead to the dawn of a morning that's bright.

SATURDAY—NOVEMBER 29.

DURING the war, Percy Lake, of 12 Hillsleigh Road, Newcastle, was a ship's cook at Scapa Flow.

He and some mates used to go ashore to the village of Holm. Straight across from the jetty was the home of Mrs Anderson, and if she saw them, she always invited them to pop in for some supper. And, when the lads trooped into her kitchen, Mrs Anderson got out a big mixing-bowl, and in a twinkling there was a pile of scrumptious pancakes. Percy can picture her still, standing with her bowl and wooden spoon at the cooker, dropping spoonfuls of the mixture on to the hot-plate. "She'd three or four lovely children," he said, "and she treated us like her own." He sent me £1 and asked me to use it to brighten someone's day, in memory of all the days Mrs Anderson and her pancakes brightened for him.

Wartime was grim, to be sure. But isn't it odd that so many of us treasure a precious memory from those dark days?

SUNDAY—NOVEMBER 30.

EVERY tree is known by his own fruit. For of thorns men do not gather figs, nor of a bramble bush gather they grapes.

DECEMBER

MONDAY—DECEMBER 1.

MR O'BRIEN passed on years ago and his friendly, cheery widow has kept on alone in the little house on the outskirts of Dublin.

Good health has always been a blessing to Mrs O'Brien who worked hard, and brought up four boys, all now married. Last year, however, she had to spend an odd day or two in bed. That could have been awkward for a body living alone, but not for Mrs O'Brien—the neighbours fussed after her, did the chores, brought what she needed, shared the gossip, and the semi-invalid had a rare old time. As she said herself, " Sure, I'm happy as a lark, and it's myself that's to blame if I'm not. I never have to say *please* to my neighbours, but seem to spend my life saying *thank you* !"

Mrs O'Brien, bless her, added, " Faith, it's wonderful." But isn't it those who love much who are much loved ?

TUESDAY—DECEMBER 2.

THOMAS CARLYLE, the famous Scottish writer, lived for a time in Chelsea, London, and became a figure of interest to the conductor of the omnibus in which the famous man often travelled. The conductor was never tired of pointing him out.

" That's Thomas Carlyle, the famous writer," he said, nudging a passenger. The other was unimpressed, however, and replied, " What an old green hat he is wearing."

" Ah," rejoined the conductor, " but think of the head beneath the hat." It is easy to judge by appearances and just as easy to be wrong.

WEDNESDAY—DECEMBER 3.

WELL, yes, perhaps I've scored a point
Or two in life's odd game.
You think I've done not badly? Well,
I differ, all the same.
For only I can know (not you)
The great things that I hoped to do!

THURSDAY—DECEMBER 4.

WOULD you keep a scrap of paper for 34 years? John Borland, of Duke's Road, Rutherglen, was taken prisoner at St Valery in 1940. As he was marched off he stopped and picked up a piece of paper fluttering across his path.

It was headed " Good News For All Men." On it were readings from the Bible, " The Lord bless thee and keep thee " ; " Whatsoever things are good " ; " Let not thy heart be troubled," and so on. John would probably just have thrown it away again if he'd found it before his army days. But he put it in his pocket.

He read it as he marched 400 miles to Germany. He read it in the cattle truck that took him to a P.O.W. camp in Poland. And he read it again and again in the five, long weary years he spent there. In the rigours of the prison camp he came to realise that for him at least, the faith it enshrined was the only thing that made sense. He organised services in the hut, singing old hymns and using his piece of paper as a Bible. Men turned to him with their problems, and he found he was able to help.

When he went home at the end of the war that scrap of paper went, too, and today you will find it safely tucked into his Bible, his proudest possession. And John? Well, he has never stopped helping people because of the faith he found at St Valery.

FRIDAY—DECEMBER 5.

ONCE a teacher had in her class a wee girl who was not very bright and not really particularly attractive.

The teacher realised the child of seven was unhappy, and that her unhappiness helped to make her dull and unsure in her work.

So she began making a point every day of sitting by her, saying a word of praise about her work and just as she left her, smiling as she whispered, " You know, you're growing prettier every day !"

At first what the teacher said was a downright lie. But the odd thing is, within a few months it was the truth ! The child blossomed as a flower.

A kindly word at the right time and in the right ear really *can* work magic !

SATURDAY—DECEMBER 6.

LITTLE Jesus wast Thou shy
Once, and just so small as I?
And what did it feel like to be,
Out of heaven and just like me?
Didst Thou sometimes think of there,
And ask where all the angels were?
I should think that I would cry
For my house all made of sky;
I would look about the air
And wonder where my angels were . . .

Francis Thompson was a great thinker, but nothing the poet wrote appeals to me more than these simple lines.

SUNDAY—DECEMBER 7.

THE Lord watch between me and thee, when we are absent one from another.

MONDAY—DECEMBER 8.

JAMES FERGUSON, a famous astronomer who died in 1776, was one of the cleverest and most kindly men Scotland has produced.

He began life as a very poor laddie, became a shepherd, and intrigued his master because he taught himself astronomy and made an astronomical map. A clergyman helped and encouraged the remarkable boy; but it was Sir John Dunbar who really set Jimmy's feet on the path to fame.

Eventually James Ferguson went to London where he painted portraits and made an astronomical diagram of the solar system. A tremendously popular lecturer on scientific subjects, he was awarded £50 a year by George the Third.

When he died he left a very large sum of money. But best of all he never forgot the people who had helped him along the hard road to fame—the farmer and the clergyman who encouraged him, and Sir John Dunbar who was such a friend in need. Not every successful man remembers old friends.

TUESDAY—DECEMBER 9.

TRULY great men and women are always ready to do little kindnesses if they can.

I am thinking particularly of the pioneer of modern surgery, Lord Lister. Although tired after operating for some hours, he paused as he came out of the theatre in a Glasgow hospital to listen to a small girl who asked him to operate on her dolly.

Lord Lister could quite easily have brushed the little girl aside, but there and then he pretended to perform an operation, and deftly sewed up the patient to prevent the stuffing coming out, before handing her back to her grateful owner.

Such is the calibre of great men.

THE FRIENDSHIP BOOK

THE things you see on your TV
Sure make you wonder if
The whole world's bad as well as mad—
Maybe it scares you stiff.
But what you rarely get is news
To warm your heart each day:
The gentle, loving things folk do,
The kindly things they say.
The worst brings fear and doubt to mind.
The hidden best is hard to find.

AT 415 Nitshill Road, Glasgow, you'll find a new block of flats.

All are two-apartment, specially for old or single people. In one of the flats lives Mrs Cornes. Some time ago she came home from Philipshill Hospital after a serious knee operation. She couldn't walk very well but it didn't keep her away from church, dear me, no!

Just off the entrance hall is a little room which the caretaker has furnished with a carpet, chairs and tables. Every Sunday, old people who cannot travel to church gather in the room, and a minister comes round to take a wee service there. There are prayers, a short sermon and hymns. Then, after the blessing, the caretaker makes a cup of tea for them all before they go.

A lovely idea, isn't it? And the thing is that the caretaker does all this for them even though he is not of their religion.

And I'm sure it doesn't matter too much whether they turn up in Sunday best or apron and slippers, so long as the heart tries to be faithful and the soul sincere.

FRIDAY—DECEMBER 12.

HOW would you judge the success or failure of a man's life?

Before you answer, listen to the story of Joe, who served for 30 years in a store in the American mid-West. One day Joe wasn't in his usual place. A customer asked about him.

" Joe's gone," said the owner of the store. " Gone?" echoed the customer. " But who'll you get to fill the vacancy?"

The store owner shrugged his shoulders. " Nobody," he said. " Joe didn't leave no vacancy."

Yes, maybe the measure of a man's success in life depends on one thing—how much he is missed when he dies. Fame and fortune have nothing to do with that. Humour, loyalty, kindliness, warmth and sincerity have everything to do with it.

Joe didn't leave no vacancy . . . Could there be a more terrible or tragic epitaph than that?

SATURDAY—DECEMBER 13.

THE kiwi, native of New Zealand, is well known as the bird that can't fly.

The reason for this is that the kiwi forages for its food on the ground, and, having no need to fly, it has gradually, through the ages, lost the use of its wings.

It's the same with any gift that we have been born with and don't use. All of us have a talent for something—although it may not be recognised as such—like making a home, saying a comforting word, lending a helping hand when needed, babysitting to let a young couple out for an evening.

Don't neglect your talent, whatever it is, or you, too, will be like the kiwi and find your talent has disappeared.

SUNDAY—DECEMBER 14.

SET your affection on things above, not on things on the earth.

MONDAY—DECEMBER 15.

A FEW years ago a friend in Edinburgh heard a young man with a fine platform presence singing at a function. His name's Michael Gerrie, and my friend was so impressed with Michael's voice he and I went into a huddle.

The upshot was that Michael started taking singing lessons and since then he has done very well. He's in great demand for concerts, and won a top award at the Edinburgh Music Festival. Now, at 23, Michael is a social work assistant at the Simon Square Centre in Edinburgh, and he's working hard to take full qualifications so that he can devote his life to helping handicapped people.

What's so unusual about that, you may ask. Well, Michael's blind. He's been so since birth. And yet he sees very clearly what path to take.

Doesn't it make you ashamed to grumble?

TUESDAY—DECEMBER 16.

IN the early days of radio, just as the first Christmas broadcast by King George V was about to begin, it was discovered a wire was loose. There was no time to attach it in the intricate set-up, and a young Post Office employee took one end of the wire in one hand and the other end in the other.

And so the speech of the King was relayed through the body of the young lad, who must have felt proud, knowing how indispensable he was. To be needed is indeed a wonderful feeling.

THE FRIENDSHIP BOOK

THE lively music of Jim MacLeod and his band is popular all over Scotland. One of Jim's greatest fans is Mrs Larg, who lives in Glen Prosen, Angus.

Mrs Larg is over 90 and unable to go and hear her favourite band. One evening her daughter happened to be dining in the hotel where Jim was appearing, and she told him all about her mother.

Next day she answered a knock at the door to find Jim MacLeod himself. He had come to visit old Mrs Larg, and after he had introduced himself the rest of the band walked in.

They all had tea, and then to Mrs Larg's delight they played for her for over an hour. All her favourite tunes. Not only that, but Mrs Larg now has one of their new L.P. records, signed by all her visitors.

Jim MacLeod and his band will be remembered, not only for their music, but for their kindness, by at least one very appreciative old lady.

NEIGHBOURS of ours sold their car recently and bought another.

Their old one was a Mini, somewhat elderly. Their new one, two years old and gleaming as brightly as the day it left the showroom, is quite a bit larger. When Daddy brought it home for the first time, wee Karen, who's four, stood looking at it thoughtfully.

" How old is it?" she asked. " Two years," said Daddy proudly.

Karen's eyes widened. " Goodness," she gasped, " isn't it big for its age?"

FRIDAY—DECEMBER 19.

NOW Christmas is a good excuse
For making others glad,
For doing lovely secret things,
And comforting the sad,
For playing Father Christmas to
Some folk who may feel cold,
Some child who'd love to be surprised,
Somebody now grown old.
Please light somebody's star and see,
How bright your Christmas-time could be.

SATURDAY—DECEMBER 20.

THE other day I bought the Lady of the House's Christmas gift—something she's always wanted. Now I prowled round the house looking for somewhere to hide it. Not my hankie drawer —she'd be sure to find it. Not the desk or the top of the wardrobe. Inside the piano? Ridiculous! Finally, I thought of the very place—behind the encyclopaedias in the bookcase. I carefully removed the two middle volumes—and there, carefully wrapped in Christmas paper, was the Lady of the House's gift to me! So I settled for the piano after all . . .

What makes two grown people behave like this in order to take the other by surprise, I cannot say. But, whatever it is, I'm sure it's something that lies close to the secret of happiness.

A Merry Christmas to you all!

SUNDAY—DECEMBER 21.

EVERY man according as he purposeth in his heart, so let him give; not grudgingly, or of necessity: for God loveth a cheerful giver.

THE FRIENDSHIP BOOK

MONDAY—DECEMBER 22.

S INCE Christmas comes but once a year,
Let's make this Christmas glad,
In spite of all there is to fear,
And much to make us sad.
May joy and happiness abound,
May song and laughter both resound!

TUESDAY—DECEMBER 23.

THE custom of having a Christmas tree goes back to the 16th century when Martin Luther was the guest of a German prince. Early on Christmas Eve he saw a tall tree in the grounds which seemed tipped by a bright star, so he cut down a small fir, brought it indoors, put candles on the branches, lit them, and invited the children to come and see it. They were wild with delight, the candle at the top looking just like the star the Wise Men saw in the East. When the Prince and Princess came in they, too, were thrilled, and next morning they placed the children's gifts under the tree.

From that time the Christmas tree gradually became a common sight all over the world at Christmas.

WEDNESDAY—DECEMBER 24.

A FRIEND of ours was thanking her little boy for his Christmas present, a somewhat garishly crayoned calendar.

" Do you *really* like it?" the boy asked, as she tacked it up on to the wall.

" Oh, yes," she said. " It's lovely. I always like *any* present I get, whether I like it or not!"

It may have sounded odd, but I think we all know what she meant!

THURSDAY—DECEMBER 25.

WITH stars to show us all the way
To Bethlehem the Blest,
With greetings, gifts and hymns—and with
The well-beloved Guest
To fill our hearts with love, we pray:
" Lord, dwell in us on Christmas Day!"

FRIDAY—DECEMBER 26.

A BOOKLET arrived for me from my friend, John Birkbeck. In it are testimonies from people who are leaders in their field — doctors, professors, politicians, and also one from a Polish woman, Helena Massalska, a " home-maker."

I find this word challenging. Usually the term is " housewife," but I do like the new word better. A house isn't always a home, after all. A housewife can make four meals a day, keep the place like a new pin, organise her family with clockwork efficiency, and be the pride of the neighbourhood. And still her house is not a home.

But a home-maker—ah, there's no doubt there. Perhaps it isn't so tidy as the house next door. Maybe, more often than not, chaos reigns. Yet when anyone walks in there's no mistaking it's a home, not simply a house.

There's a world of difference.

SATURDAY—DECEMBER 27.

WHEN days are dark and nights are chill
We sigh for summer's heat.
We sigh—and all we get, of course,
Are chilblains on cold feet!
But though bad-tempered and in pain,
We know warm days will come again!

SUNDAY—DECEMBER 28.

GLORY to God in the highest, and on earth peace, goodwill toward men.

MONDAY—DECEMBER 29.

THE spirit of Christmas is still alive and very real.

Betty Hogben, a student nurse at Sefton Hospital, Liverpool, told me this story about Jimmy Sullivan, dying from an incurable illness, yet always cheerful.

But one evening when Betty went to say good-night to him she found him in tears. He'd promised his son, 12, a bike for Christmas. The boy had talked of nothing else for weeks. And now there was no bike, and no money to buy one.

Next morning Betty told other nurses what had happened. "There are only five of us," said Sister. "We'd never manage it—still, let's club together and buy something."

Then the miracle happened. Somehow the word of Jimmy's bike spread. A stream of callers arrived at the ward. A wee student nurse who said she'd decided to slim and gave her dinner money. The porter. The cleaners. The young house doctor and the surgeon. Next day the envelope held £25!

So on Christmas Eve a brand new bike was wheeled into the ward and propped against Jimmy's locker. With the nurses' help he managed to write a card to fasten to the shining handlebars. And on Christmas afternoon, when his wife arrived with his son, there was no prouder, happier man in the hospital.

That's the end of the story—except, on that very night, while a wee boy slept with his new bike by his bed, Jimmy Sullivan slipped quietly away, a smile on his face.

TUESDAY—DECEMBER 30.

AFTER a typhoon had struck in Jamaica, a farmer and his wife were cut off by swollen rivers. The bridges and power lines were down, and after days of battling against heavy odds the farmer made a brave attempt to negotiate the floods at the narrowest point, and returned with some supplies.

Dad was greeted with cheers from his four children, one of whom, their second daughter, Tammy, rushed to carry up a parcel, slipped as she reached the back door, and had a deep gash in her leg, blood flowing quickly.

The farmer's wife instinctively picked up the telephone. Her husband shouted, " The phone's dead !"

Even as he spoke a voice said, " Hello, can I help ?"

It was not the doctor—it was a telephone repair man working on the cable. He said the water was forty feet deep, and rising ! The linesman got through to a doctor, who said he would wait till they got Tammy to him—which they somehow managed to do. And they got her back, too . . . after 13 stitches !

When it was all over, the farmer tried to ring the friendly linesman, but the phone was dead.

It all sounds melodramatic, but it is all true— and just goes to remind us that sometimes the impossible *does* happen !

WEDNESDAY—DECEMBER 31.

NEVER a Christmas morning,
Never the Old Year ends,
But someone thinks of someone,
Old days, old times, old friends.

Where the Photographs were taken

TIME TO CHAT—*Fingest Village, Bucks.*

THE TRICK — *Holtye Common, Sussex.*

IN MINIATURE — *Dymchurch-Hythe Railway, New Romney, Kent.*

MORNING MILKING — *Island of Eigg, Inverness-shire.*

A HOUSE WITH A VIEW — *Near Abernyte, Perthshire.*

LUNCH TIME — *At the ford, Kersey, Suffolk.*

THE LESSON — *Ceres, Fife.*

HARVEST TIME — *Craigrothie, Fife.*

MERRY MAY— *Hazlemere, High Wycombe.*

NATURE'S PALETTE — *In the Surrey Hills.*

SETTING OFF — *Bridge of Tilt, Perthshire.*

EARLIEST MEMORIES — *Ockle Ford, Ardnamurchan, Argyllshire.*

REVERIE — *Beaconsfield, Bucks.*

SKILL OF GENERATIONS — *Kirkcudbrightshire.*

PATIENCE — *West Worthing, Sussex.*

SPIRIT OF THE HILLS — *Ben Lui.*

IN ROMAN DAYS — *Roman Baths, Bath, Somerset.*

INSPIRATION — *Salisbury Cathedral.*

A DAY TO REMEMBER — *Kynance Cove, Cornwall.*

NEWS ! NEWS ! — *Town Crier, West Drayton.*

Printed and Published by D. C. THOMSON & Co., LTD.
12 Fetter Lane, Fleet Street, London, E.C.4.
© D. C. Thomson & Co., Ltd., 1974.